KT-571-570

Healthy Cooking
for busy people

Books are to be returned on or before

D.

055155

THE HENLEY COLLEGE LIBRARY

Healthy Cooking

for busy people

APPLE

Contents

Recipe list

Introduction

We live in an age when every aspect of our lives has been sped up, and we all seem to have less time to do anything. There are many one-parent families and families where both parents go to work, and more young people whose careers are so competitive that their working hours seem to eat away at much of their leisure time. Time to sit around a table for a shared meal seems impossible, and regular mealtimes seem like distant memories.

The Complete Book of Fast Meals is a cookbook that helps you to eat well even if your time is limited. There are dishes that take a few minutes to prepare and a few minutes to cook and there are others that are ready quickly but have a slightly longer cooking time. During that time, however, I'm sure a moment to sit down and enjoy a glass of wine, to ease back from yet another frantic day, would be welcome!

You'll find dishes in this book that can be enjoyed by anyone from children and teenagers to busy adults and those who would rather not spend forever in the kitchen. Specific starters have not been included, although there are a few desserts. However, there is no reason why one of the salads, or indeed a soup, could not be used as a starter.

Because the food in this book is fast doesn't mean that it's not good for you. A meal prepared in a few minutes can be just as tasty and nutritious as one that takes a couple of hours in the kitchen, battling through the latest trendy gourmet recipe book. Don't feel guilty using canned products, such as tomatoes or tuna in brine, as these, combined with fresh ingredients, can form the basis for some great dishes. A meal prepared from this book at home will usually be far better than grabbing a take-home meal from the local Chinese, Indian or hamburger restaurant or zapping a frozen packaged meal in the microwave.

To keep these recipes simple and quick it is important to be prepared. Before making any of the recipes in this book, read them through and make sure that you have the ingredients to hand, or that you will be able to pick them up during the day. It is also recommended that you keep a few key ingredients in your pantry, particularly canned foods such as tomatoes, tuna, a variety of beans and corn. Extra virgin olive oil and some sunflower oil or vegetable oil are essential; stocks, tomato paste, vinegars, Asian sauces (such as soy and oyster) are also basic necessities. Pasta, couscous and rice store well for absolutely ages and form the basis for many recipes in this book and indeed for much of modern-day cookery. Although fresh herbs are quite often featured in this book, a small quantity of dried mixed herbs, oregano and sweet basil will always be useful if the fresh varieties are hard to come by. Jars of olives, artichoke hearts, pesto and sun-dried tomatoes are also useful for things like pasta sauces. Finally, a reasonable selection of spices will always come in handy, especially chili or cayenne, cinnamon, turmeric, cumin and a good-quality curry powder.

If you can't get fresh produce, which should always be the first choice when buying fruit or vegetables, then commercially frozen vegetables are the next best choice. Frozen versions of hard-to-buy items such as bean shoots or other Asian varieties are sometimes the only way to go. The fresher the produce, the better it is for you, and therefore frozen vegetables, which are frozen immediately after harvesting, are going to be better for you than vegetables that have been lying around in your local corner store for a week or more!

There are dishes in this book that will suit any occasion, whether it is something for the kids, something for a cold winter's night, or a dish to impress friends. Some of the recipes can be made in advance and frozen. Other dishes can be stored in the refrigerator for a few days.

Considering the ease with which these recipes can be made, it can be confidently recommended that you try to eat at least one home-cooked meal a day—best served at the table. This way of eating is good for your digestion, so you'll get the maximum benefit from whatever you eat. It also enables you to enjoy and share the pleasure of eating and conversation with your family or friends.

The well-stocked kitchen

It is possible to make appealing meals from a few items in your cupboards, supplemented with a few things from the local store or deli. A well-stocked pantry and small supply of a few fresh, refrigerated items provide the basis for impromptu, hassle-free meals. The recipes in this book are based on the idea of minimum effort, and take into account that most of us don't have a kitchen full of fresh produce because we haven't had time to shop for a week.

It's a good idea to plan a few menus in advance and purchase in bulk the food you use frequently. If you stock your kitchen with staples, these will form the basis of many interesting meals when added to a minimal amount of readily available fresh ingredients.

Herbs, spices and seasonings
- plant pots or a mini garden with a few essentials—chives, parsley, basil, cilantro (coriander)
- dried herbs—oregano, thyme, sage, rosemary, dill, bay leaves
- spices—salt, black pepper, ground cinnamon, nutmeg, mixed spice, chili flakes or cayenne pepper, paprika, cumin, fennel or caraway seeds
- exotic extras—Mexican-style chili powder, Chinese five-spice powder, garam masala, curry paste

Stocks
- fish, chicken, beef or vegetable in cartons or frozen, cubes (bouillon) or powder, canned consommé

Sauces, condiments and dressings
- savory sauces—Worcestershire, Tabasco, ketchup (tomato sauce)
- Oriental extras—mirin or sake (substitute dry sherry), soy, hot or sweet chili, oyster
- condiments—honey, fruit chutney, marmalade, redcurrant jelly, Dijon and English mustards, gherkin relish, mint sauce, tomato salsa
- dressings—egg mayonnaise, vinegar (red or white wine, cider or malt), oil (vegetable or peanut, olive)

Canned and packaged goods
- whole peeled tomatoes, tuna or salmon, condensed soups, coconut cream, tomato paste (concentrate), evaporated milk, red kidney or cannellini beans, pineapple pieces
- delicatessen delicacies—anchovy fillets, capers, marinated artichoke hearts or olives, sun-dried tomatoes

Fresh produce
- for flavoring—onions, garlic, ginger, lemons
- for salads—celery, green or red bell pepper (capsicum), scallions (shallots/spring onions), red (Spanish) onion, cucumber, assorted salad leaves
- everyday standbys—tomatoes, potatoes, carrots, frozen green peas, frozen spinach

Refrigerated items
- milk, cream, butter, cooking margarine, eggs, cheese (including parmesan, cheddar), yogurt or sour cream, bacon

Basic staples
- flour—all-purpose (plain), self-rising (self-raising)
- sugar—granulated, superfine (caster), confectioners (icing); soft brown (light and dark)
- baking basics—leavening (baking powder, bicarbonate of soda/baking soda), cocoa powder or cooking chocolate, unsweetened shredded (desiccated) coconut, vanilla extract (essence)
- dried fruit—apricots, golden raisins (sultanas), dates
- thickeners—cornstarch (cornflour) or arrowroot
- coatings—dried breadcrumbs, soda crackers (saltines)
- cereals—bread, rice (white, brown), pasta (including elbow macaroni, spaghetti), polenta (yellow cornmeal), cracked wheat (burghul), couscous
- nuts and seeds—pine nuts, walnuts, blanched flaked almonds, sesame seeds

Equipment

Basic cooking equipment is a must if you are pushed for time. Having the right implement to hand will mean you are not looking for a substitute. Below is a guide to some of the items you should keep in your kitchen, so you are ready to whip up a meal at a moment's notice.

Hand tools

- knives—paring (long and short-bladed, one serrated), cleaver (chopper), carver
- graduated measuring spoons and cups, 2-cup jug, scales (optional), slotted spoon, tongs, wooden spoons, spaghetti spoon (optional), eggflip (pancake turner), whisk, meat fork, ladle, kitchen shears, flexible-bladed metal spatulas (long and short), rubber spatula (scraper), flat fish server, can opener, potato masher, vegetable peeler, apple corer

Utensils

- mixing—glass or metal bowls of graduated sizes
- baking—oven gloves or cloth, sifter or sieve, baking sheets, pie pan (flan ring) with removable base, fluted quiche dish, pie dishes (1 fruit plate, 1 oval dish for meat), springform or round cake pans, square pan, muffin pan, loaf pan, wire cooling rack
- roasting—roasting pan, roasting rack, baking dish with lid, meat thermometer
- stove-top cooking—saucepans with lids: small (with pouring spout), medium and large, double boiler insert (or heatproof bowl to fit pan), deep-fry basket insert (optional); frying pans (large and small, nonstick), crepe/omelette pan, oval fish poacher/kettle (optional), wok and wok chan, flameproof casserole dish with lid (preferably cast iron)

Accessories

- paper towels, foil, greaseproof (waxed) paper, baking (parchment) paper, plastic food wrap and bags
- 2–3 cutting boards
- citrus juicer
- screw-top jar for dressings, salad bowl and servers
- sieve (1 small, 1 large), colander
- metal steamer insert or bamboo or metal steamer
- grater (shredder)
- bamboo and metal skewers, toothpicks, kitchen string
- brushes for pastry and basting
- ramekins for use in microwave (for melting, etc.)
- egg rings, egg poacher (optional)

Appliances

- hand-held electric mixer, small blender, standard food processor

How to cook…

To cook perfect pasta

1. Use lots and lots of water so that the pasta can move around. Bring to a rapid boil and keep boiling, even when adding pasta. Add a dash of olive oil and a pinch of salt.

2. Add all the pasta at once, stir to ensure none of it is sticking together, and continue to stir regularly throughout cooking.

3. Do not overcook. Check the pasta a few minutes before you think it will be done and keep checking until it is al dente (meaning it offers only just a little resistance when bitten).

4. Drain quickly in a colander and run a little water through. Serve immediately.

Cooking time depends on the shape and size of the pasta. If you can't serve it straight away, toss with a little olive oil to keep moist. You should do this if you are storing leftover pasta too. If you need to keep the pasta warm, return it to the dry but warm pan and cover. To reheat already-cooked pasta, add it to freshly boiling water for about 30 seconds.

Fresh pasta keeps for a few days in the refrigerator. Dried pasta keeps almost indefinitely.

Great rice

There is a variety of white rice available, including long-grain, short-grain, and arborio rice, and perfumed long-grain rices such as basmati and jasmine. There is also wild rice which is not a rice at all, but a kind of aquatic sea grass. Store white rice in a sealed container in a cool, dark place; it will keep for over a year. Brown rice will keep for a few months if stored in the refrigerator.

Most rice can be cooked using the absorption method. For each cup of rice, use the indicated amount of water: medium to long-grain rice—$1^3/_4$–2 cups, short-grain rice—$1^1/_2$–2 cups, basmati—$1^1/_2$ cups.

First, rinse rice well. Place in a saucepan with water and bring mixture to the boil over high heat. Stir once, cover tightly, and reduce heat to low. Cook according to the time indicated on the packet, usually 15 to 20 minutes, without lifting lid. If all water has not been absorbed, cover again and cook for a few more minutes. When done, fluff rice with a fork and let stand, covered for a few minutes off the heat.

Try cooking rice in stock or adding herbs to the cooking water for added flavor.

Classic mashed potato

Peel and cut big floury potatoes in quarters and place in cold salted water to cover. Bring to the boil and cook covered until tender, about 20–30 minutes. Test with a skewer. Drain, then return to hot saucepan and leave for a couple of minutes until extra moisture evaporates, shaking occasionally. Add hot milk, butter, salt, and pepper and mash with a fork until smooth. If you like your potatoes extra creamy, beat with a wooden spoon.

Try adding a finely chopped white onion or scallion and a chopped garlic clove while mashing. Or add grated gruyere or cheddar cheese. Be really decadent and use hot bacon fat instead of butter when mashing!

Dried beans

Pulses is the general name for dried beans, peas, and lentils. They make a great basis for a meal as they are inexpensive, simple to prepare, very filling, and high in protein. Some of the most popular are:

- haricot or white beans—these include navy beans, soissons, and flageolets
- cannellini beans
- butter or lima beans
- borlotti beans
- chick peas, ceci peas, or garbanzo beans
- red kidney beans
- broad or fava beans
- black-eyed beans or peas.

You can store dried pulses, tightly sealed, in a dark, dry place for up to a year. You can also buy most pulses already prepared and canned, which reduces time and effort.

To cook, rinse thoroughly first and sort out any undesirable pieces. Cover with water and soak for several hours or overnight. Rinse, then cover with fresh water in a saucepan and simmer until tender. You can add garlic, bay leaves, chili, or other spices but don't add salt, sugar, or acids (such as tomatoes) until after cooking, as this can toughen the beans.

Dried lentils need no presoaking, and small red lentils only take about 15 minutes to cook. Brown and green lentils take a little longer. Place in a saucepan with enough cold water to cover. Bring to the boil then simmer until just tender, not mushy.

soups

Bean and pasta soup

Preparation: 10 minutes
Cooking time: 45–50 minutes
Serves: 4–6

1 onion, sliced

3 sticks celery, sliced

4 slices smoked streaky bacon, rinded and chopped

1 tablespoon olive oil

5 cups (40 fl oz/1.25 L) beef stock

1 cup (6 oz/175 g) cooked or canned black-eye
beans

1 cup (6 oz/175 g) cooked or canned lima (butter)
    beans

30 oz (75 g) pipe rigate pasta

salt and freshly ground black pepper

Fry onion, celery and bacon in oil in large pan for 2 to
3 minutes. Add stock and beans, bring to the boil, cover
the pan and simmer for 30 minutes.

Add pasta to the pan and cook for a further 10 to
15 minutes, until pasta is tender. Season to taste.

Tips
• Try using other beans, such as cannellini, borlotti or
  red kidney beans, or a combination of three or four.

Borsch

Preparation: 15 minutes

Cooking time: 55 minutes

Serves: 4–6

1 purple onion, chopped

1 lb (450 g) lean braising steak (chuck, blade), cut
into small cubes

1–2 tablespoons oil

1 lb (450 g) raw beets (beetroot), peeled and grated

12 oz (350 g) red cabbage, finely shredded

5 cups (40 fl oz/1.25 L) beef stock

2 tablespoons red wine vinegar

1 tablespoon ketchup (tomato sauce)

salt and freshly ground black pepper

1 teaspoon dried thyme

8 oz (250 g) firm waxy potatoes, peeled and diced

½ cup (4 fl oz/125 ml) low-fat sour cream

1 teaspoon fennel seeds, to serve

2 teaspoons chopped fresh dill, to serve

Cook onion and beef in oil in a large covered pan until beef is brown. Add beets, cabbage, stock, vinegar, ketchup, salt, pepper and thyme. Bring to a boil, reduce heat and simmer for 40 minutes.

Add potatoes to pan and cook for a further 10 minutes.

Divide the soup among six warmed bowls. Put
1 tablespoon sour cream into the middle of each, then sprinkle with fennel seeds and dill.

THE HENLEY COLLEGE LIBRARY

Chinese noodle soup

Preparation: 2 minutes

Cooking time: 5 minutes

Serves: 4

12 cups (96 fl oz/3 L) chicken stock

8 oz (250 g) Chinese egg noodles, cooked

4–8 tablespoons soy sauce

4 tablespoons oyster sauce

salt, to taste

2–4 tablespoons dry sherry, (optional)

chili to taste (either chopped fresh, minced from the
  jar, or as sauce or paste)

4 cups (24 oz/750 g) chicken, cooked and shredded

Heat stock in a saucepan. If using dry noodles, boil them
in the stock for a few minutes or according to packet
directions. Add soy and oyster sauces, salt, and sherry.
Taste and adjust seasonings as required.
Add chili.

Place chicken in four soup bowls. Pour stock and noodles
over each and serve hot.

Tips

• Add ¼ teaspoon or more freshly grated ginger.

• Add a dash of sesame oil.

• Top with chopped scallions (shallots/spring onions) and
  cilantro (coriander) leaves.

• Add ¼ cup chopped ham.

• Add some Chinese greens (cabbage or bok choy, for
  example) or steamed broccoli to broth while heating.

• Use rice noodles instead of egg noodles, if you prefer.

Chunky vegetable soup

Preparation: 10 minutes
Cooking time: 25–30 minutes
Serves: 4–6

2 large onions
2 cloves garlic
1 stick celery
1 tablespoon olive oil
3 cups (24 fl oz/750 ml) tomato or mixed vegetable juice
3 cups (24 fl oz/750 ml) chicken or vegetable stock
6 unpeeled small new potatoes
8 oz (250 g) young turnips
1 lb (500 g) carrots or young parsnips, or a combination
4 unpeeled zucchini (courgettes)
6–8 small yellow squash
1/2 cup (2 oz/60 g) frozen peas or whole corn kernels
2–3 sprigs fresh parsley, chopped
2 tablespoon chopped fresh basil or 1 teaspoon dried
freshly ground black pepper
crusty bread, to serve

Peel and chop onion and garlic. Trim and chop celery. Heat oil in a large, heavy-based saucepan over medium heat and cook onion, garlic and celery, stirring, for 5 minutes or until golden. Add juice and stock to pan and bring to boil.

Cut potatoes and turnips into 1-inch (2.5-cm) chunks and add to pan. Reduce heat and simmer for 12 to 15 minutes, or until vegetables are almost tender.

Meanwhile, peel and dice carrots or parsnips into 1/2-inch (1-cm) cubes. Trim ends from zucchini, halve or quarter lengthwise and thickly slice. Halve and thickly slice squash.

Add vegetables to pan with peas, parsley, basil and pepper to taste. Simmer, stirring occasionally, for 10 minutes or until vegetables are tender.

Serve in heated deep soup plates with crusty bread.

Clam chowder

Preparation: 5 minutes

Cooking time: 25 minutes

Serves: 2–4

14 oz (440 g) canned clams, undrained

2 rashers bacon, chopped

1 small onion, chopped

3 large potatoes (about 3 cups), peeled and diced

salt and white pepper

1½ cups (12 fl oz/375 ml) fish stock or water

½ cup (4 oz/125 g) light whipping cream

½ cup milk

Remove clams from liquid; reserve 1½ cups of the liquid. Chop clams into small chunks.

Fry bacon in saucepan over low heat until crisp. Add onion and sauté over medium heat until soft. Add potatoes and toss through. Add salt and pepper, reserved clam liquid, and stock. Simmer for 15 minutes, until potatoes are tender.

Add clams, cream and milk, and gently heat through. Let stand if possible (see below). Reheat if necessary and serve warm.

Tips

- Chowder improves with standing, so if you have time, let it stand off the heat for 1 hour or refrigerate it overnight before reheating.

- Serve topped with fresh chopped chives or thyme and freshly ground black pepper.

- Salted crackers are the traditional accompaniment.

- You may like to add a handful of finely chopped celery, green bell pepper (capsicum), and/or carrot with the potatoes.

- Corn chowder can be made by using canned corn kernels instead of clams, and vegetable or chicken stock instead of fish stock.

Cream of spinach soup

Preparation: 2 minutes

Cooking time: 20 minutes

Serves: 4

3 packs (about 1½ lb/750 g) frozen spinach, chopped
2 tablespoons (1 oz/30 g) butter or olive oil
1 small onion, finely chopped
1 clove garlic, finely chopped
2 tablespoons all-purpose (plain) flour
4 cups (32 fl oz/1 L) chicken stock
salt and pepper to taste
½ teaspoon nutmeg, or to taste
1 cup (8 fl oz/250 ml) light whipping cream
cayenne pepper or hot pepper sauce to taste, to
  serve

Place frozen spinach in a saucepan, cover, and cook gently for 10 minutes or until softened. Drain well and transfer to a food processor.

Place butter, onion and garlic in saucepan and cook until onion is soft. Sprinkle in flour, and stir until onion is golden. Add stock and boil for 5 minutes, stirring.

Add half this liquid to spinach in food processor and puree until smooth. Return this mixture to the saucepan and season with salt, pepper, and nutmeg. Add cream and heat gently—do not boil.

Serve with a sprinkle of cayenne or a dash of hot pepper sauce.

Tips

• Smoked salmon, chopped or cut into thin strips, can be scattered on top.

• If you prefer something more flavorsome, try adding spices with the onion: 1 teaspoon ground cumin, 2 teaspoons mustard seeds, 2 teaspoons chopped ginger, 1 chopped garlic clove, 1 chopped red chili.

• Experiment with the taste of fenugreek, cloves, and cinnamon—¼ teaspoon of any of these is a place to start.

Gazpacho

Preparation: 10 minutes
Chilling time: 20 minutes
Serves: 2

1 can (13 oz/400 g) tomatoes, drained
1 cup (8 fl oz/250 ml) tomato juice
2 teaspoons balsamic or white wine vinegar
1 tablespoon olive oil
1/2 red bell pepper (capsicum), seeded and finely chopped
1/2 small purple onion, finely chopped
1 small cucumber, finely diced
7 oz (210 g) cooked shrimp (prawns), peeled and chopped
1 tablespoon chopped fresh parsley
1/2 small avocado, peeled and diced

Combine tomatoes, juice, vinegar and oil in food processor and puree until smooth. Chill for at least 20 minutes.

Stir in remaining ingredients and serve.

Hearty potato and salami soup

Preparation: 10 minutes

Cooking time: 25 minutes

Serves: 4

7 oz (210 g) spicy salami, finely diced

1 tablespoon olive oil

1 large onion, chopped

2 cloves garlic, minced

2 lb (1 kg) potatoes, peeled and cut into ¾-inch (2-cm) cubes

1 medium carrot, chopped

6 cups (48 fl oz/1.5 L) chicken stock

1 bunch fresh English spinach, stemmed and shredded

Cook salami in dry frying pan over medium-high heat until browned. Drain on paper towels.

Heat oil in same pan over medium heat. Add onion and garlic and cook, stirring, until onion is soft. Add potatoes, carrot and stock. Simmer, uncovered, until potatoes and carrots are tender, 10 to 15 minutes.

Add spinach and stir over heat until wilted. Stir in salami and serve hot.

Miso soup

Preparation: 10 minutes

Cooking time: 15 minutes

Serves: 3–4

7 oz (220 g) Asian-style noodles

2 tablespoons miso (soy bean paste)

5 cups (40 fl oz/1.25 L) boiling water

1 chicken breast (about 7 oz/210 g), cut into small
   pieces

¼ small leek or 3 scallions (shallots/spring onions),
   cut into strips

5 oz (150 g) chopped English spinach leaves

1 zucchini (courgette), cut into strips

3 button mushrooms, sliced

¼ cup (½ oz/15 g) freshly chopped cilantro
   (coriander) leaves or flat-leaf parsley, to serve

Cook noodles according to directions. Drain and set aside.

Combine miso and water in saucepan and stir over medium heat to dissolve paste. Add remaining ingredients except coriander and simmer over medium heat for10 minutes or until chicken is cooked through.

Add cooked noodles and reheat. Serve sprinkled with cilantro or parsley.

Tips
• Flavor this soup with just about anything from the fridge—any leftover vegetables can be added.

• Once the paste is dissolved, you can add the remaining soup ingredients at leisure.

Mushroom soup

Preparation: 10 minutes

Cooking time: 15 minutes

Serves: 2

1 teaspoon olive oil

1 slice bacon, most fat removed, finely chopped

3 scallions (spring onions/shallots), chopped

7 oz (210 g) mixed mushrooms

4 cups (32 fl oz/1 L) chicken stock

2 tablespoons chopped fresh parsley

salt and freshly ground pepper

1 cup (2 oz/60 g) cooked small pasta

4 slices thick bread

4 slices gruyère cheese

Heat oil in saucepan (preferably nonstick) over medium heat. Add bacon, scallions and mushrooms and cook, partially covered, for 5 to 10 minutes, stirring occasionally.

Add stock and bring to boil. Stir in parsley, salt and pepper to taste, and cooked pasta.

Top each slice of bread with piece of cheese and broil (grill) until cheese melts. Serve immediately with hot soup.

Tips

• Choose any type of mushroom or use a variety — oyster mushrooms, wild mushrooms, large cultivated field mushrooms. Button mushrooms are just as delicious as any.

Parsley fish soup

Preparation: 15 minutes

Cooking time: 20 minutes

Serves: 4

1 onion, chopped

1 oz (30 g) low-fat polyunsaturated margarine

8 oz (250 g) potatoes, peeled and diced

2½ cups (20 fl oz/600 ml) fish stock

1½ cups (12 fl oz/375 ml) low-fat (skimmed) milk

salt and freshly ground black pepper

1 lb (500 g) boneless, skinless flounder (plaice or sole)

1 oz (30 g) parsley, stalks removed

2 tablespoons thickened cream or heavy (double) cream

In a large pan, cook the onion in margarine until soft, then add potatoes, stock, milk, salt and pepper and three-quarters of the fish. Bring to a boil, cover pan and simmer gently for 10 to 15 minutes, just until potatoes are soft.

Transfer soup to a blender or food processor, add parsley and blend until smooth. Return soup to pan.

Cut the remaining quarter of the fish into thin strips and add to the pan with the cream. Reheat gently and simmer for 2 to 3 minutes, until fish strips are cooked. Serve in warmed soup bowls.

Peasant bean soup

Preparation: 5 minutes

Cooking time: 25 minutes

Serves: 4

1 tablespoon olive oil

2 cloves garlic, chopped

1 large onion, chopped

14 oz (440 g) can peeled tomatoes, undrained

13 oz (400 g) can borlotti beans

4 cups (32 fl oz/1 L) chicken stock

1/4 cup (2 oz/60 g) tomato paste

1 teaspoon dried thyme or 2 teaspoons fresh thyme

1 teaspoon dried basil or 1 tablespoon fresh basil

1 bay leaf

4 oz (125 g) pasta

Place oil, garlic, and onion in a deep, heavy-bottomed saucepan and cook over medium heat until onion is soft. Add tomatoes with juice, break up roughly, and cook for a couple of minutes. Add beans, stock, tomato paste and herbs and simmer gently for 10 minutes. Add pasta and simmer until soft, about 5 to 10 minutes.

Tips

• For pasta, use either long threads such as spaghetti broken into pieces or small shapes such as elbow macaroni.

• Serve with freshly grated parmesan.

• Substitute any kind of bean: red kidney, cannellini, black-eyed peas, even a can of mixed beans.

• If you don't have stock, use 2 undrained cans peeled tomatoes and 1/2 cup water.

• Try a sliced leek instead of the onion.

• Use 1/2 teaspoon ground coriander instead of thyme, and add 1 teaspoon chili powder (or to taste).

• Add chopped bacon with the onions.

• Add 1 cup roughly chopped fresh spinach or curly endive.

• Instead of beans and pasta, mash 1 large potato and stir it through the soup. Throw in a handful of black olives.

Potato and watercress soup

Preparation: 15–20 minutes

Cooking time: 40 minutes

Serves: 6

2 oz (60 g) butter or margarine

8 scallions (shallots/spring onions), trimmed and
  sliced

12 oz (375 g) potatoes, peeled and diced

2 bunches watercress, trimmed and roughly
chopped

3 cups (24 fl oz/750 ml) chicken or vegetable stock

salt and freshly ground black pepper

1/2 teaspoon Worcestershire sauce

2 teaspoons lemon juice

1 1/4 cups (10 fl oz/300 ml) milk

6 tablespoons light (single) cream

6 tablespoons plain (natural) yogurt

watercress sprigs, to serve

Melt butter in a large saucepan and sauté scallions and
potato gently for a few minutes without browning. Add
watercress to pan and toss. Add stock, seasonings,
Worcestershire sauce and lemon juice and bring to boil.
Cover and simmer gently for about 30 minutes, until
tender.

Cool slightly and either sieve the soup or puree in a
blender or food processor and return to a clean pan. Stir
in milk and bring back to a boil for about 1 minute.

Thoroughly blend cream and yogurt, and add about half
to the soup. Reheat gently and adjust seasonings.

Serve each portion with a spoonful of the remaining
cream and yogurt mixture swirled through it and topped
with watercress sprigs.

Tip

For a chilled soup, cool and then chill thoroughly after
pureeing. Stir in the cream and yogurt before serving.

Quick beef and pepper soup

Preparation: 10 minutes
Cooking time: 35 minutes
Serves: 4

2 tablespoons olive oil
1 onion, chopped
12 oz (375 g) lean braising steak (chuck or blade),
    cut into very small dice
1 tablespoon paprika
1 footer Florence fennel, about 8 oz (250 g), cut into
    small dice
salt and freshly ground black pepper
4 cups (32 fl oz/1 L) beef stock
1 large red bell pepper (capsicum), seeded and cut
    into diamond shapes

1 large yellow bell pepper (capsicum), seeded and
    cut into diamond shapes
2 tablespoons chopped fresh parsley, to serve

Heat oil in a large saucepan and sauté onion for about
2 minutes, until soft. Add beef and cook until browned.
Stir in paprika, fennel, salt, pepper and stock and bring
to a boil. Cover pan, reduce heat and simmer for
20 minutes.

Add bell peppers and cook for a further 10 minutes.
Divide soup among four warmed soup bowls and
sprinkle with chopped parsley.

Simple onion soup

Preparation: 5 minutes

Cooking time: 50 minutes

Serves: 4–6

3 tablespoons butter

1 lb (500 g) onions, thinly sliced

1 cup (8 fl oz/250 ml) dry white wine

½ cup (4 fl oz/125 ml) water

5 cups (40 fl oz/1.25 L) beef or chicken stock

salt and freshly ground black pepper

baguettes (French breadsticks), sliced and toasted,
  to serve

gruyère cheese, freshly grated, to serve

Melt butter in a deep, heavy-bottomed pan. Add onions, wine, and water and cook very gently on low heat until onions are soft, about 30 to 40 minutes, stirring regularly. Add stock and season to taste. Bring to a boil, cover, and simmer 10 minutes.

Meanwhile, top toasted bread with grated cheese and broil (grill) until cheese is melted and golden.

Divide soup among individual bowls, and top each with a slice or two of bread. Serve immediately.

Tips

- If you love cheese, you may like to add loads of gruyère and maybe a bit of parmesan on top.

- You can also place unmelted cheese and toast on top of the individual soup bowls and then pop the whole lot under the broiler (grill) so that the entire top is covered with cheese.

Smoked chicken and pumpkin soup

Preparation: 10 minutes

Cooking time: 35 minutes

Serves: 2

1 tablespoon olive oil

1 small onion, finely chopped

grated zest of 1 lemon or 1-inch (2.5-cm) piece
lemongrass, finely chopped

3 fresh cilantro (coriander) roots, chopped (optional)

1 clove garlic, minced

1 teaspoon grated fresh ginger

1 lb (500 g) peeled pumpkin, cut into 1-inch (2.5-cm)
cubes

3 cups (24 fl oz/750 ml) chicken stock

5 oz (150 g) smoked chicken breast, cut into pieces

chopped scallions (shallots/spring onions) or fresh
cilantro (coriander) leaves, to serve

Heat oil in a saucepan over low heat. Add onion, lemon zest, coriander root, garlic and ginger and cook, stirring, 3 to 4 minutes. Add pumpkin and cook, stirring, for 2 to 3 minutes. Add stock, bring to a boil and simmer until pumpkin is tender, about 15 minutes. Let cool slightly.

Puree mixture in a blender or food processor. Return to the saucepan, add chicken and heat through.

Serve garnished with scallions.

Tips

- This recipe makes good use of the fresh cilantro (coriander) you can buy in bunches; the roots can be used to add flavor. Don't use the "hairy" part of the root—just the fleshy end of the stalks.

- Smoked chicken can be bought at delicatessens.

- Cutting the pumpkin into smaller pieces reduces cooking time.

Smoked ham minestrone served with pesto

Preparation: 10 minutes

Cooking time: 40 minutes

Serves: 4

8 oz (250 g) small pasta shells

¼ cup (2 fl oz/60 ml) olive oil

8 oz (250 g) carrots, diced

8 oz (250 g) onions, chopped

2 cloves garlic, minced

2 celery stalks, chopped

8 oz (250 g) zucchini (courgettes), diced

4 oz (125 g) smoked ham, diced

2–3 cups (16–24 fl oz/500–750 ml) vegetable stock

1 can (13 oz/400 g) cannellini beans, rinsed and drained

8 oz (250 g) broccoli florets

8 oz (250 g) green beans, sliced

¼ cup (2 fl oz/60 ml) prepared pesto, to serve

Half-cook pasta in boiling salted water 5 minutes; drain.

Heat oil in a large saucepan over medium heat. Add carrots, onion, garlic and celery and cook, stirring, until onion is soft, about 5 minutes. Add zucchini and ham with just enough cold stock to cover. Bring to a boil, then reduce heat and simmer until vegetables are just tender, about 10 minutes. Add drained beans and cook for 5 minutes. Stir in broccoli and green beans and simmer for 5 minutes. Stir in half-cooked pasta and simmer until tender, about 5 more minutes.

Serve soup with a dollop of pesto swirled through.

Spicy corn and tomato soup

Preparation: 10 minutes

Cooking time: 35 minutes

Serves: 4

1 tablespoon vegetable oil

1 medium onion, chopped

2 cloves garlic, pressed (crushed)

1 celery stalk, chopped

grated zest and juice of 1 orange

½–1 teaspoon Tabasco or other hot pepper sauce,
  or to taste

2 lb (1 kg) ripe plum (egg) tomatoes, chopped

8 oz (250 g) chorizo sausage, sliced

13 oz (400 g) can creamed corn

4 oz (125 g) corn chips

2 oz (60 g) sharp cheddar

Heat oil in a saucepan. Add onion and cook, stirring, until soft. Stir in garlic and celery and cook, stirring, until celery is soft. Add orange zest and juice, Tabasco and tomatoes and simmer, covered, for 20 minutes.

While soup is simmering, cook sausage in an ungreased frying pan until lightly browned. Drain.

Blend or process tomato mixture until finely chopped. Stir in corn, return to pan and heat through.

Just before serving, spread corn chips in broiler (grill) pan. Sprinkle with cheese and place under broiler (grill) just until cheese melts.

Stir chorizo into soup and serve with corn chips.

Tomato and coconut soup

Preparation: 2 minutes

Cooking time: 10 minutes

Serves: 2–4

2 x 14 oz (440 g) cans tomatoes, with juice

2 teaspoons sugar

1 teaspoon salt

2 tablespoons plain (all-purpose) flour

1 tablespoon vegetable oil

2 teaspoons ground cilantro (coriander)

2 teaspoons cumin

½ teaspoon (or to taste) cayenne pepper or chili powder

1 cup (8 fl oz/250 ml) coconut cream (thick)

black pepper, freshly ground

Puree tomatoes with sugar, salt, and flour in a blender or food processor.

Heat oil in a saucepan and cook spices until fragrant, about 1 minute. Add coconut cream and pureed tomatoes. Simmer, stirring, for a few minutes until slightly thickened. Season with pepper to taste.

Tips

- Serve sprinkled with chopped fresh cilantro (coriander) leaves or basil.

- Instead of the spices, use 1 teaspoon each crushed garlic and ginger. Then add a tablespoon of chili sauce and a dash of teriyaki sauce with the coconut cream.

- For a curried corn and tomato soup, follow the basic recipe but instead of the spices use 1 teaspoon crushed garlic, 2 teaspoons curry powder, and 1 small onion, chopped. Then add a 5 oz/150 g can of corn kernels with the coconut cream.

- You can use 1 oz (30 g) creamed coconut dissolved in 1 cup water instead of the coconut cream.

Vichyssoise

Preparation: 15 minutes
Cooking time: 40 minutes
Serves: 6

3 tablespoons (1½ oz/40 g) butter or margarine
3 large leeks, trimmed of most green and finely
    sliced
1 onion, peeled and thinly sliced
1 lb (500 g) potatoes, peeled and diced
3¾ cups (30 fl oz/900 ml) chicken or vegetable stock
salt and white pepper
¼ level teaspoon ground cilantro (coriander)
1 egg yolk
⅔ cup (5 fl oz/150 ml) light (single) cream
snipped chives, to serve

Melt butter in a large saucepan and sauté leek and onion very gently for about 5 minutes, without browning. Add potato, stock and seasonings and cilantro and bring to a boil. Cover and simmer gently for about 30 minutes, or until vegetables are very tender.

Cool a little, then sieve or puree the soup in a blender or food processor and pour into a clean saucepan.

Blend the egg yolk with cream and whisk evenly into the soup. Reheat gently without boiling, adjust seasonings, cool, then chill thoroughly.

Serve sprinkled liberally with snipped chives.

Tips
- This classic dish may also be served hot—simply serve after reheating.

Zucchini broth

Preparation: 5 minutes
Cooking time: 30 minutes
Serves: 4

1 tablespoon olive oil
2 cloves garlic, crushed
2 onions, thinly sliced
4 large zucchini (courgettes), very thinly sliced
6 cups (48 fl oz/1.5 L) chicken stock
pinch salt
black pepper, freshly ground
parmesan, freshly grated, to serve

Place olive oil and garlic in a saucepan over low heat and cook until garlic is fragrant. Add onions, stir, and cook for a few minutes, until they soften. Stir in zucchini and cook for 5 to 10 minutes, until zucchini softens. Add a third of the stock and simmer gently for 5 minutes. Add salt, pepper, and remaining stock, and simmer for another 5 to 10 minutes so that zucchini is very soft but not falling apart.

Serve with freshly grated parmesan sprinkled on top.

salads

Eggplant and tahini salad

Preparation: 15 minutes plus 30 minutes standing

Cooking time: 5 minutes

Serves: 4

1½ lb (750 g) eggplants (aubergines)

salt

3 tablespoons olive oil

1 clove garlic, crushed

½ cup (2 oz/60 g) black olives

1 tablespoon wine vinegar

2 tablespoons tahini (sesame seed paste)

2 tablespoons plain (natural) yogurt

1 tablespoon lemon juice

fresh cilantro (coriander) leaves, to serve

Cut the eggplants into thick slices, then again into thick sticks. Put them into a large sieve and sprinkle with salt. Let stand for 30 minutes, rinse with cold water, then dry on paper towels.

Heat olive oil in a large pan and fry the eggplant, stirring constantly, until soft and lightly browned. Add garlic, olives and vinegar to the pan and mix well. Transfer to a serving dish. Let stand until cold.

Mix together the tahini, yogurt and lemon juice. Drop teaspoonfuls of the mixture over the salad and garnish with the coriander leaves.

Tips

• The salting of the eggplants ensures that all the bitter juices are drained off.

• Tahini is a crushed sesame seed paste that is available from large supermarkets and specialty food stores.

Feta and couscous salad

Preparation: 10 minutes

Cooking time: 5 minutes

Serves: 2

1 cup (6½ oz/200 g) couscous

2 cups (16 fl oz/500 ml) boiling water

4 oz (125 g) feta cheese, cubed

2 tablespoons olive oil

1 tablespoon lemon juice

½ small purple onion, sliced

1 cucumber, sliced

1 tablespoon each chopped fresh mint, parsley and
  dill

selection of meats, to serve

4 small pita breads, warmed, to serve

store-bought hummus, to serve

Place couscous in a bowl or saucepan that has a lid
and pour boiling water over. Cover and let stand for
5 minutes. Fluff with fork. Gently stir in feta, oil, juice,
onion, cucumber and herbs.

Serve salad on platter with selection of meats, warm pita
bread and hummus.

Tip

Serve the salad with a selection of cold cuts from the
deli—pastrami, prosciutto and smoked ham, for
example.

Green salad with vinaigrette

Preparation: 5–10 minutes

Serves: 4

1 clove garlic

1 teaspoon Dijon mustard

pinch of sugar

freshly ground black pepper

1 tablespoon white or red wine vinegar or lemon juice

1/4–1/3 cup (2–3 fl oz/60–90 ml) virgin olive oil

4–6 cups mixed fresh salad leaves (see below)

1 small red (Spanish) onion

1 tablespoon chopped fresh or 1/2 teaspoon dried
    herb, e.g. basil, thyme, tarragon, chives, mint

For the dressing, peel and halve the garlic. Place all ingredients in a screw-top jar. Cover and shake until blended. Or, whisk together first 5 ingredients in a small bowl. Gradually add oil, whisking constantly, until dressing thickens slightly. Stand dressing at room temperature to develop flavors, while preparing salad ingredients. Remove garlic and shake or whisk again before serving.

Tear salad leaves into bite-size pieces and place in a salad bowl. Peel onion, slice thinly and separate into rings. Scatter onion and herbs, if using, over salad and mix lightly to combine.

Pour dressing over salad, toss lightly and serve immediately.

Tips

- Choose an interesting mix of salad lettuces and leaves for color, flavor and texture. Look for mixed salad leaves
at the store—some include edible flower petals, e.g. nasturtiums, marigolds, violets.

- Try adding some of the following for extra interest and bulk:
    — blanched and refreshed snow peas (mange tout),

    — marinated artichoke hearts, black or stuffed green olives, sun-dried tomatoes or bell peppers (capsicum) in oil, canned anchovy fillets, crumbled feta, goat cheese or sliced bocconcini (fresh mozzarella);

    — sliced grilled beef, leg ham, cooked chicken or turkey, poached fish or canned tuna, hard-cooked (boiled) eggs (hen or quail), canned chickpeas (garbanzo beans), red kidney or cannellini beans;

    — toasted nuts, croûtons.

- For a robust garlic flavor, finely chop garlic and let it infuse in oil for 1 to 2 hours before preparing dressing.

- Generally, the ratio of vinegar to oil is one part vinegar to three parts oil; however, you may prefer more or less oil.

- Experiment with a variety of oils and vinegars, including those already flavored with herbs.

Grilled chicken salad with sour cream dressing

Preparation: 10 minutes

Cooking time: 30 minutes

Serves: 2

1 tablespoon white wine vinegar

2 tablespoons olive oil

2 tablespoons sour cream

1 teaspoon Dijon mustard

1 clove garlic, minced

salt and freshly ground pepper

6 small new potatoes, halved

2 tablespoons olive oil

1 whole chicken breast (about 13 oz/400 g)

2 slices bacon, chopped

2 small tomatoes, chopped

5 oz (150 g) baby spinach or arugula (rocket) leaves

1 avocado, peeled and chopped

For dressing, combine vinegar, olive oil, sour cream, Dijon mustard, garlic and salt and pepper and whisk until smooth. Set aside.

Boil potatoes until tender. Drain and keep warm.

Meanwhile, heat 1 tablespoon oil on a barbecue or stovetop grill or in a heavy-based frying pan. Cook chicken breast over medium heat about 5 minutes on each side. Let cool slightly, then cut into pieces.

Place chicken in a large bowl and pour ½ the dressing over.

Heat remaining olive oil and fry bacon until crisp. Add to chicken with tomato, spinach and avocado, and toss with remaining dressing.

Serve with potatoes.

Grilled halloumi cheese platter

Preparation: 10 minutes

Cooking time: 5 minutes

Serves: 2

8 oz (250 g) halloumi cheese, cut into slices ½ inch
   (1 cm) thick

2 teaspoons olive oil

freshly ground pepper

2 tablespoons lemon juice

2 tablespoons store-bought tapenade (olive paste)

½ bunch (about 5 oz/150 g) arugula (rocket) leaves

2 plum (egg) tomatoes, sliced

1 small hothouse (continental) cucumber, sliced

½ cup (2 oz/60 g) combined chopped fresh mint and
   basil leaves

4 store-bought dolmades

lemon wedges, to serve

1 tablespoon olive oil, to serve

Brush each side of cheese slices with a little olive oil and
sprinkle with pepper. Heat frying pan or barbecue or
stovetop grill and cook cheese for 2 minutes on each
side, sprinkling with lemon juice and additional pepper.

Arrange cheese on plate with salad ingredients and
drizzle with olive oil.

Tips

• Halloumi is a Greek cheese that is quite salty. Some
  varieties come in sealed packages that keep for weeks
  in the refrigerator, and are handy to have on hand.

• Dolmades are rice-stuffed grape vine leaves that are a
  popular appetizer in the Mediterranean region.

• The tapenade, dolmades and halloumi are all available
  from delicatessens and Middle Eastern markets—ask
  for a variety of halloumi that you can grill.

Grilled pepper salad

Preparation: 10 minutes plus cooling time
Cooking time: 5 minutes
Serves: 4–6

2 large red bell peppers (capsicums)
2 large green bell peppers (capscicums)
2 large yellow bell peppers (capsicums)
3 tablespoons olive oil
1 clove garlic, crushed
salt and freshly ground black pepper

Cut the bell peppers into quarters; discard the seeds. Lay on a baking sheet skin side up. Broil (grill) until the skin begins to turn black and blister. Remove from heat, let stand until cool enough to handle, peel off the skin.

Cut each piece of bell pepper in half again. Arrange in a shallow dish.

Mix the olive oil with the garlic, salt and pepper. Pour over the bell peppers.

Tips

• Bell peppers can be prepared up to one day in advance. Keep covered in the refrigerator but bring to room temperature to serve.

• Omit the yellow bell pepper and arrange the red and green bell peppers with some sliced yellow tomatoes when available.

Marinated bean salad

Preparation: 5–10 minutes

Cooking time: 5–6 minutes

Serves: 6–8

6 oz (180 g) fresh green beans

6 oz (180 g) fresh yellow wax beans

14 oz (400 g) can red kidney beans

14 oz (400 g) can chickpeas (garbanzo beans)

10 oz (300 g) can cannellini or lima beans

1 small green bell pepper (capsicum)

1 purple onion

2 tablespoon chopped fresh parsley

1/3 cup (3 oz/90 g) sugar

1/3 cup (3 fl oz/90 ml) vegetable oil

2/3 cup (51/2 fl oz/150 ml) cider vinegar

1/2 teaspoon salt

1/4 teaspoon freshly ground black pepper

Tips

- For extra flavor, cover and refrigerate dressed beans, stirring once or twice, for 6 to 8 hours or overnight. Note: Use a non-metallic—glass, ceramic or plastic—bowl or container for marinating and storing, as a metal container may react with the vinegar to create a metallic taste.

- The tangy-sweet dressing makes this a tasty side dish for glazed barbecued chicken, sausages and pork spareribs.

- If yellow wax beans aren't available, double the quantity of green beans.

- Return leftover salad to reserved dressing, cover and refrigerate for up to 1 week.

Trim stem ends from fresh beans. Cut beans diagonally into 2-inch (5-cm) lengths. Place in a steamer basket over simmering water in a saucepan, cover and steam 5 to 6 minutes or until beans are just tender. Drain and refresh under cold running water. Place in a non-metallic bowl.

Drain canned beans and peas in a colander and rinse. Drain well and add to fresh beans.

Halve bell pepper, remove seeds and cut into 1/4-inch (5-mm) pieces. Peel and finely chop onion. Add with parsley to bean mixture.

To make dressing, place sugar, oil, vinegar, salt and pepper in a bowl and stir until blended. Pour over beans and mix well.

To serve, stir beans in dressing to coat. Drain well, reserving dressing, and serve.

Marinated tomatoes

Preparation: 10–60 minutes
Serves: 2–4

8 basil leaves, chopped
1 clove garlic, finely chopped
4 tablespoons extra virgin olive oil
8 ripe red tomatoes, chopped roughly
2 cups (8 oz/250 g) ricotta cheese
bread, pita bread, or pasta, to serve

Combine basil, garlic, and oil. Pour over tomatoes and let stand for up to 1 hour (10 minutes will do).

Pile ricotta on top and serve at room temperature with the accompaniment of your choice.

Variations

- You can eat the tomatoes with slices of dense bread or torn pieces of pita bread, toasted under the broiler (grill).

- Try tossing tomato and ricotta (still at room temperature) through hot pasta.

- If serving as a salad with bread, you could add 2 teaspoons balsamic or red wine vinegar to the oil mixture if desired.

- Leave out the ricotta and pile the tomatoes on top of toasted Italian bread—you have the beloved Italian dish, bruschetta.

- If you can be bothered, this will taste even better if you skin the tomatoes. Make a cross with a knife at the bottom end and then place them in a bowl of extremely hot water for 5 minutes. Remove, allow to cool a little, then peel off the skins.

- Cottage cheese can provide a handy substitute for ricotta.

Mediterranean pasta salad

Preparation: 10 minutes

Cooking time: 30 minutes

Serves: 4

8 plum (egg) tomatoes

2 cloves garlic, minced

3 tablespoons olive oil

2 tablespoons balsamic vinegar

¼ cup (1 oz/30 g) chopped fresh basil leaves

6 slices pancetta

1 large purple onion, sliced

8 oz (250 g) goat cheese

1 lb (500 g) pasta, cooked and drained

Heat oven to 325°F (160°C/Gas 3). Cut tomatoes in half and arrange on baking sheet. Combine garlic, 2 tablespoons oil, vinegar and ½ of the basil in a small bowl and mix well. Spoon a little of the oil mixture onto each tomato. Broil (grill) tomatoes under low heat for 30 minutes.

Broil (grill) pancetta until crisp, about 1 minute on each side. Toss onion in remaining tablespoon of oil, arrange slices on baking sheet and broil (grill) under high heat for 2 minutes or until slightly softened and lightly browned.

Cut goat cheese into ½-inch (1-cm) cubes. Toss pasta with cheese, onion and remaining basil. Top with tomatoes and pancetta. Serve warm or cool.

Oriental noodle salad

Preparation: 10 minutes

Cooking time: 15 minutes

Serves: 2

½ cup (4 fl oz/125 ml) coconut milk

2 teaspoons fish sauce

2 teaspoons palm sugar or brown sugar

2 teaspoons rice wine or white wine vinegar

1 teaspoon finely grated ginger

1 small red chili, chopped finely

1 clove garlic, minced

about 12 oz (375 g) Asian-style noodles

10 oz (300 g) chicken thigh fillets

3 scallions (shallots/spring onions), cut into
  1-inch (2.5-cm) strips

½ cup (1 oz/30 g) fresh cilantro (coriander) leaves

1 cucumber, sliced

3 oz (90 g) snow peas (mange tout), blanched and
  sliced

½ red bell pepper (capsicum), seeded and thinly sliced

For dressing, whisk together coconut milk, fish sauce, sugar, vinegar, ginger, chili and garlic. Set aside.

Cook noodles according to package instructions. Drain and set aside.

Meanwhile, grill or broil chicken for 4 to 5 minutes each side, until cooked through. Let cool slightly. Slice and combine with cooked noodles and remaining ingredients while still warm.

Stir through dressing and serve immediately.

Tips

• This dressing is good over any salad that includes cooked fish or meats, such as peeled shrimp (prawns), salmon pieces or strips of beef.

• Use any sort of Asian-style noodle—these are usually cooked for a few minutes in boiling water.

• If you don't have a really large bowl, you can use a wok to serve the noodle salad.

Pear and watercress salad

Preparation: 15 minutes
Serves: 4

1 bunch watercress
4 ripe pears, peeled and cored
30 oz (90 g) creamy blue cheese
2 tablespoons unflavored (natural) Greek yogurt
1 tablespoon vegetable oil
freshly ground black pepper
1 bunch scallions (shallots/spring onions), chopped

Line a round serving plate with the watercress. Slice the pears and arrange in overlapping slices over the watercress.

Crumble the blue cheese into the yogurt, add the oil and pepper. beat well then pour over the pears. Sprinkle with the scallions and serve immediately.

Tips

• This salad can be prepared 2 to 3 hours in advance, but if you do this, brush the pear slices with lemon juice to prevent them from going brown.

• Suitable cheeses for this salad are Dolcelatte, Bleu de Bresse and Pipo Cream.

Vinaigrette dressing

1 clove garlic
1 tspn Dijon mustard
pinch of sugar
freshly ground black pepper
1 tblspn white or red wine vinegar or lemon juice
1/4–1/3 cup (2–3 fl oz/60–90 ml) virgin olive oil

Peel and halve garlic. Place all ingredients in a screw-top jar. Cover and shake until blended. Or, whisk together first 5 ingredients in a small bowl. Gradually add oil, whisking constantly, until dressing thickens slightly. Stand dressing at room temperature to develop flavors, while preparing salad ingredients. Remove garlic and shake or whisk again before serving.

Potato salad

Preparation: 8 minutes
Cooking time: 10–12 minutes
Refrigeration time: 1 hour
Serves: 6–8

2 lb (1 kg) small new potatoes
vinaigrette dressing (see below)
2 sticks celery
4 scallions (shallots/spring onions) with some green tops
1 cup (8 fl oz/250 ml) mayonnaise
1/2 cup (4 fl oz/125 ml) sour cream
1 1/2 teaspoons Dijon mustard or horseradish cream
freshly ground black pepper
fresh parsley, chopped, to serve

Place potatoes in a saucepan of lightly salted water to cover, bring to a boil, and cook for 10 to 12 minutes, or until just tender. Drain and cool until easy to handle. Peel, if desired, and cut into thick pieces.

Place warm potatoes in a bowl, drizzle with vinaigrette and toss lightly to coat. Cover and refrigerate for 1 to 2 hours, or until cold.

Trim and slice celery and scallions and add to potatoes.

Combine mayonnaise, sour cream and mustard in a bowl. Season to taste with black pepper. Lightly fold mixture through potatoes. Refrigerate until required. Serve well chilled, sprinkled with parsley.

Tips

• Choose a waxy, red-skinned potato that keeps its shape when cooked. Avoid overcooking—potatoes should be just tender when pierced with a skewer.

• Omit garlic from vinaigrette dressing for milder flavor. Add fresh dill or chives instead.

• Add 6 to 8 sliced stuffed green olives or 1 to 2 chopped or sliced hard-cooked (boiled) eggs, if desired.

• Make salad ahead and refrigerate, covered, overnight to let flavors mingle.

Radicchio and garlic mushroom salad

Preparation: 5 minutes

Cooking time: 10 minutes

Serves: 4

12 large wild mushrooms, field mushrooms or very
  large open button mushrooms

3 tablespoons olive oil

2 cloves garlic, minced

1 tablespoon chopped fresh parsley

3 slices bacon, chopped

1 head radicchio

4 oz (125 g) shaved parmesan, to serve

2 oz (60 g) pine nuts, toasted, to serve

12 cherry tomatoes, halved, to serve

Place mushrooms under broiler (grill) top side up, and cook for 1 minute. Turn mushrooms over. Combine oil, garlic and parsley and sprinkle mixture on mushrooms. Cook mushrooms for 3 more minutes or until tender.

Cook bacon in dry frying pan until lightly browned and crisp. Arrange radicchio leaves among four plates. Place 3 mushrooms on each. Sprinkle with bacon, parmesan and pine nuts. Dot plates with cherry tomatoes.

Rice or pasta salad

Preparation: 8–10 minutes
Cooking time: 10–12 minutes
Serves: 1–2 hours

8 oz (250 g) long-grain white or brown rice, or small
 pasta shapes such as penne, spirals, elbows, shells
double quantity vinaigrette dressing (see p. 44)
1 purple onion
2–3 sticks celery
4–6 radishes
8–10 black olives, pitted (stoned)
8–10 cherry tomatoes
4 tablespoon chopped fresh parsley
lettuce leaves, to serve

Cook rice or pasta in a large saucepan of lightly salted boiling water until tender but still slightly firm to the bite. Drain well. If using pasta, rinse under cold running water and drain again. Transfer to a salad bowl.

Prepare vinaigrette and combine with rice or pasta.

Peel and thinly slice or finely chop onion. Trim and slice celery and radishes. Halve or thickly slice olives and tomatoes. Add vegetables and chopped parsley to bowl. Toss lightly, cover and refrigerate for 1 to 2 hours.

To serve, arrange lettuce in a shallow serving plate or bowl and spoon salad over.

Tips

- Flavors improve if dressing is mixed with warm rice or pasta.

- For a main course salad, add any of the following before serving: diced or slivered cooked ham or chicken, drained can of tuna in brine, sliced hard-cooked (boiled) eggs, or toasted pine nuts, walnuts or pecans.

- A little fruit is delicious in a rice salad: golden raisins, chopped dried apricots, canned pineapple pieces, fresh orange segments, or diced unpeeled apple.

Salad nicoise

Preparation: 5 minutes

Cooking time: 20 minutes

Serves: 4

10 whole baby (new) potatoes or 5 large, cut in
quarters

7 oz (200 g) frozen broad (fava) beans

4 tomatoes, cut into wedges

2 x 7 oz (200 g) canned tuna, drained and flaked with
a fork

4 anchovy fillets

½ cup (2 oz/70 g) black olives

4 eggs, hard-cooked (boiled)

Dressing

1 tablespoon white wine vinegar

6 tablespoons extra virgin olive oil

juice of 1 lemon

big pinch salt

Boil potatoes until tender, about 15 to 20 minutes; drain
and cool slightly.

Meanwhile, cook beans until tender; drain and cool
slightly.

Place potatoes and beans in a bowl with tomatoes and
tuna.

Mix dressing ingredients. Pour desired amount over
salad and toss lightly.

Top with anchovies, olives, and eggs. Serve while still
slightly warm or at room temperature.

Tips

• Use roma (plum) tomatoes if possible, cut into thick
slices.

• Halving and roasting the tomatoes is a non-traditional
quirk that will lift this dish immeasurably.

• Add strips of roasted red pepper (capsicum) for a lively
difference.

• Use fresh green beans instead of frozen broad beans.

• Use chunks of seared fresh tuna steak instead of
canned tuna.

• Add extra bulk with salad greens.

• Aoili can be substituted for the vinaigrette dressing.

Spicy salami, potato and tuna salad

Preparation: 10 minutes

Cooking time: 25 minutes

Serves: 4

1¼ lb (625 g) waxy potatoes, peeled

3 oz (90 g) sliced spicy salami

1 large romaine (cos) or other lettuce

6 oz (180 g) canned water-packed tuna, drained

2 tablespoons chopped drained capers

½ cup (4 fl oz/125 ml) mayonnaise

2 tablespoons lemon juice

1 tablespoon tomato paste

1 tablespoon prepared pesto

6 oz (180 g) red bell pepper (capsicum), sliced

2 oz (60 g) pitted (stoned) black olives

Boil potatoes until tender; drain, cool and slice. Cut salami slices into quarters. Tear lettuce leaves.

Blend or process tuna, capers, mayonnaise, lemon juice, tomato paste and pesto until smooth.

Combine potatoes, salami, lettuce, pepper and olives in salad bowl and drizzle with dressing. Toss and serve.

Spinach and brie salad with raspberry vinaigrette

Preparation: 10 minutes

Cooking time: 10 minutes

Serves: 4

1 yellow bell pepper (capsicum)

1 bunch fresh English spinach, washed and with
  stems removed

1 small mango, peeled, pitted (stoned) and sliced

1 celery stalk, thinly sliced

3 oz (90 g) cherry tomatoes, halved

1 Asian (nashi) pear, cored and cubed

8 oz (250 g) soft, ripened brie

3/4 cup (3 oz/90 g) chopped pecans, toasted

2 teaspoons Dijon mustard

1/4 cup raspberries

2 tablespoons raspberry vinegar

2 tablespoons olive oil

Quarter pepper; remove seeds and membranes. Broil
(grill) pepper, skin side up, until skin blisters and
blackens. Transfer to plastic bag until cool enough to
handle, then peel skin away. Cut pepper into thin strips.

Combine pepper, spinach, mango, celery, tomatoes and
pear in large salad bowl.

Cut cheese into bite-size pieces and roll in chopped nuts
to coat.

Blend or process mustard, raspberries, vinegar and oil
until well combined. Just before serving, pour dressing
over salad and toss well. Dot salad with cheese and
sprinkle remaining nuts over.

Spinach salad with walnuts

Preparation: 5 minutes

Serves: 2–4

²/₃ cup (2¹/₂ oz/75 g) walnut halves

1 bunch English spinach

4 bocconcini cheese, sliced or quartered

cracked black pepper

Dressing

5 tablespoons walnut oil blended to taste with peanut
   oil

1 tablespoon red wine or raspberry vinegar

Toast walnut halves on a baking tray under a hot broiler
(grill).

Cut off tough part of stems from spinach and arrange
leaves in salad bowl.

Add bocconcini, walnuts, and pepper.

Mix dressing ingredients, pour desired quantity over the
salad and toss lightly.

Tips

- Blue cheese always works well with spinach and
  walnuts, so you could crumble some into the salad
  instead of bocconcini or make it into a dressing by
  blending to taste with a few tablespoons of olive oil,
  lemon juice, and either crème fraîche or sour cream.

- Try chunks of camembert or brie, or shavings of
  parmesan, instead of bocconcini.

- Crisp cook slices of prosciutto or bacon under the
  broiler (grill) and add to the salad.

- Toss in very thin strips of red pepper (capsicum)—
  roasted first if you like.

- Add caramelized purple onion. Cut it, unpeeled, into
  thick slices then cook under a hot broiler (grill) until very
  brown, brushing regularly with olive oil. Cool and peel
  before tossing into salad.

- Substitute other salad leaves such as arugula (rocket).

Warm main-course salad

Preparation: 15–20 minutes

Cooking time: 15 minutes

Serves: 4

12 oz (375 g) young English spinach

⅓ cup (3 fl oz/90 ml) vegetable or olive oil

½ cup (2 oz/60 g) coarsely chopped walnuts

4 slices prosciutto or bacon

1 clove garlic

2–3 tablespoon red wine vinegar or lemon juice

1 teaspoon sugar

¼ teaspoons chopped hot red chili or dried chili flakes

2 oz (60 g) goat or feta cheese, to serve

Rinse spinach under cold running water, drain and dry with paper towels. Tear larger leaves into bite-size pieces and place in a serving bowl.

To make dressing, heat oil in a frying pan over medium heat. Add walnuts and cook, stirring, for 1 minute, or until golden. Remove pan from heat. Remove nuts immediately with a slotted spoon and scatter over spinach.

Cut prosciutto into thick strips. Peel and chop garlic. Return pan to heat and cook prosciutto and garlic, stirring, for 2 to 3 minutes, or until prosciutto is crisp and golden.

Add vinegar, sugar and chili to pan and simmer, stirring, 30 seconds. Spoon dressing over salad, toss lightly and sprinkle with crumbled cheese. Serve immediately.

Tips

• Replace prosciutto or bacon with just-cooked or room temperature meat, fish or poultry.

• Serve as a first course or, with bread, as a light main meal.

• Use an assortment of lettuce leaves mixed with watercress and parsley instead of spinach, if desired. Add a few blanched and refreshed vegetables such as snow peas (mange tout), green beans or asparagus.

pasta, grains & pulses

Bacon and bean risotto

Preparation: 5 minutes
Cooking time: 20 minutes
Serves: 4

¼ cup (2 fl oz/60 ml) olive oil
2 strips bacon, chopped
6 sage leaves, chopped
3 cups (24 fl oz/750 ml) chicken or vegetable stock
2 cups (7 oz/220 g) arborio rice
14 oz (440 g) canned cannellini beans
freshly ground black pepper
parmesan, to serve (optional)

Place most of the olive oil, most of the bacon, and half the sage in a saucepan and fry over medium heat until bacon is almost cooked.

Meanwhile, bring stock to a boil in another saucepan. Add rice to saucepan with bacon and stir for a few minutes, until well coated in oil. Pour boiling stock into pan with rice, return to boil, cover, then reduce heat to low and simmer for 20 minutes.

Meanwhile, add remaining oil, bacon, and sage to a pan and fry for a couple of minutes. Add beans and simmer over very low heat until rice is ready.

Uncover rice and stir. If stock has not been fully absorbed, cover and cook for a few more minutes. Spoon onto plates then pile bean mixture on top. Grind black pepper over and add shavings of parmesan if desired. Serve immediately.

Tips

- Add a tablespoon of butter with the olive oil to risotto when you want a more buttery taste.

- For the classic northern Italian dish known as risotto alla milanese, add ¼ cup white wine to the stock, bring to boil, and add a pinch of saffron threads or ½ teaspoon powdered saffron. When rice is cooked, stir in ½ cup freshly grated parmesan and 1 tablespoon butter before serving.

- Add a tablespoon of pesto to the uncooked rice, and stir a few more spoonfuls through the cooked risotto with a drizzle of olive oil.

- Soak ½ cup dried porcini mushrooms and add with the uncooked rice.

- Fry 8 oz (250 g) chicken fillet (cut into small pieces) with the onion at the start, and add a handful of chopped sun-dried tomatoes with the uncooked rice.

- Sauté onion then add 2 chopped tomatoes and a few shredded basil leaves with the uncooked rice.

Bacon and spinach penne

Preparation: 5 minutes

Cooking time: 1 hour

Serves: 4

8 large tomatoes

2 teaspoons dried basil or oregano

2 cloves garlic, chopped

4 strips bacon, chopped

4 tablespoons olive oil

salt and freshly ground black pepper

1 bunch English spinach

1 lb (500 g) penne

Preheat oven to 400°F (200°C/Gas 6).

Cut tomatoes in half and place (cut side up) in baking dish. Scatter with basil, garlic, and bacon. Drizzle with olive oil. Season with salt and pepper. Bake for 50–60 minutes, until very soft. When tomatoes are almost done, put pasta on to boil.

Rinse spinach and remove thick stalks. Place in heavy saucepan, cover tightly, and cook over low heat, stirring frequently until it begins to wilt, about 3 minutes. Cover and cook 1 to 2 more minutes, until tender. Squeeze out extra moisture.

Drain cooked pasta and place in a large bowl. Break up tomatoes roughly and add, along with pan juices, to pasta. Add spinach and toss.

Tips

• Serve with shavings of parmesan if desired.

• Throw a handful of black olives into the baking dish as well.

• Alternatively, roast a whole head of garlic with the tomatoes for a really earthy dish.

• Instead of bacon, serve the tomatoes with slices of prosciutto that have been crisped under the broiler (grill).

• If you want to make it even simpler, forget the bacon and spinach altogether.

• Make up the tomatoes and garlic alone and serve with crusty bread, instead of pasta, to soak up the juices.

Bavette with olive oil and garlic

Preparation: 3 minutes

Cooking time: 12 minutes

Serves: 4

6 tablespoons extra virgin olive oil

5 cloves garlic, slivered

1 lb (500 g) bavette

freshly ground black pepper

parmesan shavings, to serve (optional)

chopped parsley, to serve (optional)

Place olive oil and garlic in small pan over very low heat. Heat slowly until the garlic is just turning golden brown—the oil will be infused with garlic, so you can discard all or some of the slivers if desired.

Meanwhile, cook pasta until al dente, usually 5 to 12 minutes. The moment pasta is cooked, drain and place in large serving bowl. Pour garlicky olive oil over the top and toss well.

Serve with lots of freshly ground black pepper and shavings of parmesan or chopped parsley if desired.

Tips

• You can add a sliced chili with the garlic.

• Or halve the quantity of garlic and add 4 oz (125 g) chopped anchovy fillets instead.

Bean stew with tequila salsa

Preparation: 10 minutes

Cooking time: 15–20 minutes

Serves: 4

2 cans (13 oz/400 g each) cannellini beans

1 can (13 oz/400 g) chopped tomatoes

8 cloves garlic, minced

4 sprigs oregano, chopped, or 3 teaspoons dried

½ cup (4 fl oz/125 ml) olive oil

½ small red bell pepper (capsicum), seeded and
finely diced

½ small yellow bell pepper (capsicum), seeded and
finely diced

1 small red chili, finely chopped

1 tablespoon chopped fresh cilantro (coriander)
leaves

1 tablespoon chopped fresh parsley

1 small orange, peeled and finely diced

1 lime, peeled and finely diced

¼–1 teaspoon Tabasco or other hot pepper sauce,
to taste

2 tablespoons tequila

Drain and rinse beans; mash ¼ of them. Combine
beans, tomatoes, garlic, oregano and oil in medium
saucepan over medium-low heat. Cover and cook,
stirring occasionally, until tomatoes and oil have boiled
together and mixture is slightly thickened, 15 to
20 minutes.

Combine remaining ingredients in small bowl and mix
well. Serve warm beans topped with salsa.

Beans with sage and tomato

Preparation: 5 minutes

Cooking time: 15 minutes

Serves: 2–4

3 tablespoons olive oil

2 cloves garlic, finely chopped

2 strips bacon, chopped

1 tablespoon sweet paprika

4–6 sage leaves, chopped

2 large tomatoes or 13 oz (400 g) canned tomatoes,
    chopped and drained

2 x 13 oz (400 g) cans beans

salt and freshly ground pepper

toasted bread or hot pasta, to serve

Place oil, garlic, and bacon in a saucepan and sauté until bacon is just starting to cook. Add paprika, sage, and tomatoes and cook until tomatoes are soft . Add beans and gently heat through for 5 to 10 minutes to allow the beans to absorb the flavors.

Season with salt and pepper. Serve hot with bread or pasta.

Tips

- You can use ground sage, to taste, instead of fresh, but it won't be as flavorsome.

- You can use pancetta instead of bacon, or a spicier meat such as chorizo.

- You can use dried beans, but you will have to soak them overnight.

- You can also serve this dish at room temperature with fresh bread or as part of an antipasto plate.

Conchiglie with smoked trout and lemon zest

Preparation: 5 minutes
Cooking time: 15 minutes
Serves: 2

8 oz (250 g) pasta shells
1 lemon
2 teaspoons olive oil
2 tablespoons tarragon vinegar
¾ cup (6 fl oz/180 ml) light (single) cream
½ cup (60 g/2 oz) fresh peas
½ side (5 oz/150 g) smoked trout, skin and bones
  removed
salt and freshly ground pepper
fried lemon rind, to serve

Cook pasta in large saucepan of boiling salted water until al dente.

Meanwhile, remove rind from lemon with vegetable peeler and cut into thin strips. Heat oil in frying pan and cook lemon rind over medium heat for 2 to 3 minutes, stirring, until golden. Drain on paper towels and set aside.

Boil vinegar in saucepan until reduced by half. Add cream and peas and simmer for 3 to 4 minutes. Add smoked trout and salt and pepper to taste. Simmer for 2 minutes more.

Serve immediately over drained cooked pasta sprinkled with fried lemon rind.

Crab, lime and caper pasta

Preparation: 5 minutes

Cooking time: 10–15 minutes

Serves: 2

8 oz (250 g) pasta

1 tablespoon white wine vinegar

2 scallions (spring onions/shallots), chopped

½ cup (4 fl oz/125 ml) light (single) cream

1 cup (6 oz/180 g) cooked crabmeat

grated zest of 1 lime

2 tablespoons chopped fresh cilantro (coriander) leaves

2 teaspoons drained capers

salt and freshly ground pepper

chopped fresh cilantro (coriander) leaves, to serve

Cook pasta in large saucepan of boiling salted water until al dente. Drain.

Combine vinegar and scallions in saucepan and bring to boil. Boil for 1 minute. Add all remaining ingredients except pasta and garnish and simmer for 2 minutes, or until heated through. Adjust seasoning to taste.

Serve over hot pasta, sprinkling with extra coriander if desired.

Tip

Instead of crab, you can use a drained small can of tuna or an 8 oz (250 g) white fish fillet. If using fish, first poach the fillet in ½ cup (4 fl oz/125 ml) simmering water for 3 minutes then flake, using two forks to separate the flesh.

Preheat oven to 375°F (190°C/Gas 5). Cook macaroni in a large saucepan of boiling, lightly salted water for 8 to 10 minutes (until al dente). Drain and return to pan.

Prepare a double quantity of white sauce. Stir pieces of cream cheese and mustard into sauce after milk. Cook over medium heat, stirring, until sauce is smooth and thick. Remove pan from heat. Add cheddar and stir until melted.

Pour sauce over macaroni and mix well. Spread mixture evenly in an 8 cup (64 fl oz/2 L) shallow ovenproof dish. Cut each tomato into 3 or 4 slices and arrange over macaroni.

Finely crumble bread with fingers. Combine with parsley and butter and sprinkle over tomatoes.

Bake for 20 to 25 minutes, or until mixture is bubbling and top is golden.

White sauce

Makes 1 cup (8 fl oz/250 ml)

2 tablespoons butter
2 tablespoons all-purpose (plain) flour
1 cup (8 fl oz/250 ml) warmed milk
salt and ground white or black pepper, to taste

Melt 2 tablespoons butter in a saucepan over medium heat. Add 2 tablespoons all-purpose (plain) flour and using a whisk or wooden spoon, cook stirring, for 1 minute.

Remove pan from heat. Gradually blend in 1 cup (8 fl oz/250 ml) warmed milk. Return pan to heat and cook, stirring constantly, until sauce bubbles and thickens. Season to taste with salt and ground white or black pepper.

Creamy macaroni and cheese

Preparation: 15 minutes
Cooking time: 20–25 minutes
Serves: 6

7 oz (220 g) elbow macaroni
double quantity white sauce (see below)
4 oz (125 g) cream cheese, at room temperature
2 teaspoon Dijon or wholegrain mustard
8 oz (250 g) grated cheddar
2 tomatoes
2 slices white sandwich bread, crust removed
2 tablespoon chopped fresh parsley
2 tablespoon melted butter

Farfalle with lemon

Preparation: 3 minutes

Cooking time: 15 minutes

Serves: 4

½ cup (4 fl oz/125 ml) extra virgin olive oil

2 cloves garlic, crushed

1 cup fresh parsley, chopped

4 tablespoons lemon juice

1 lb (500 g) farfalle

4 tablespoons freshly grated parmesan

freshly ground black pepper

Place oil, garlic, and parsley in small saucepan over low heat, and cook until garlic is fragrant, about 1 minute. Remove from heat, add lemon juice and set aside.

Cook pasta until al dente, usually 5 to 12 minutes. Drain, and return to warm saucepan with a dash of olive oil.

Heat lemon sauce (if necessary) and pour over pasta. Toss with parmesan and black pepper.

Tips

• A bit of lemon zest can add extra tang.

• Along with the lemon juice, add a 7 oz (220 g) can solid-packed tuna, drained and broken up with a fork. Parmesan is optional.

• If adding tuna, you may also like to add a dash of Worcestershire or hot pepper sauce and even a handful of chopped walnuts.

• Along with the lemon juice, add a 7 oz (220 g) can crabmeat, instead of tuna, drained and broken up with a fork. Do not add parmesan to this sauce.

Fettuccine with herbs, ham and parmesan

Preparation: 5 minutes

Cooking time: 10–15 minutes

Serves: 2

8 oz (250 g) fettuccine

¼ cup (2 fl oz/60 ml) white wine

⅔ cup (5½ fl oz/160 ml) light (single) cream

¼ cup (½ oz/15 g) assorted chopped fresh herbs, such as rosemary, thyme, chives, parsley, basil and mint

3½ oz (100 g) thinly sliced ham, chopped

2 tablespoons grated parmesan

salt and freshly ground pepper

Cook pasta in large saucepan of boiling salted water until al dente. Drain.

While pasta is cooking, place wine in saucepan and bring to boil. Boil until reduced by half (2 to 3 minutes). Stir in cream and return to boil. Reduce heat to simmer.

Add herbs and ham and heat through for 1 minute.

Pour sauce over hot pasta and sprinkle with parmesan. Season with salt and pepper to taste.

Tips

• You can use prosciutto instead of ham, cut into thin lengths instead of chopped.

• Use all the herb varieties suggested or choose one or two. Note that rosemary and thyme are strongly flavored herbs.

Fettuccine with roasted red peppers and artichokes

Preparation: 2 minutes

Cooking time: 20 minutes

Serves: 4

**3 large red bell peppers (capsicums), halved
lengthwise and seeded**

4 tablespoons olive oil

1 clove garlic, finely chopped

12 oz (375 g) jar marinated artichoke hearts, undrained

4 oz (125 g) canned sardines, torn into pieces

1 lb (500 g) fettuccine

black pepper, cracked, to serve

parmesan shavings, to serve (optional)

Place peppers on tray under hot broiler (grill), skin side up, and cook under high heat until the skin blackens and bubbles. Let cool slightly, peel off skin and cut peppers into strips.

Place olive oil and garlic in a pan and cook over medium heat until garlic is fragrant, about 1 minute.

Halve artichoke hearts and add to pan with 6 tablespoons marinade and red pepper strips. Sauté gently over very low heat while cooking pasta. Add sardines and heat through.

Cook pasta until al dente, usually 5 to 12 minutes. Toss with artichoke, peppers, sardines and oil. Serve with cracked pepper and parmesan shavings.

Tips

• Add a handful of chopped black olives or a dollop of tapenade for extra impact visually and on the palate.

• Instead of parmesan, crumble goat cheese on top.

• You can make a pantry-only special by tossing strips of canned pimiento pepper with the artichoke instead of fresh red pepper.

Fried rice with steamed bok choy

Preparation: 10 minutes

Cooking time: 15 minutes

Serves: 2

2 teaspoons olive oil

1 egg, beaten

1 slice bacon, chopped

1½ oz (50 g) button mushrooms, sliced

3 scallions (spring onions/shallots), cut into 1-inch (2.5-cm) pieces

1 clove garlic, minced

2 teaspoons finely grated fresh ginger

3 cups (about 10 oz/300 g) cooked long-grain rice

1 tablespoon soy sauce

2 bunches baby bok choy

salt and freshly ground pepper

extra soy sauce, to serve

Heat 1 teaspoon oil in nonstick frying pan or wok. Add egg and cook over medium heat until top begins to bubble. Gently flip and cook other side 1 to 2 minutes. Roll up, remove and chop. Set aside.

Heat remaining oil in frying pan or wok and cook bacon, mushrooms, scallions, garlic and ginger over medium heat for 3 to 4 minutes. Add rice and cook for 3 to 4 more minutes, stirring. Add soy sauce and chopped omelette.

Meanwhile, steam bok choy until tender, about 5 minutes. Season with a little salt and pepper.

Serve fried rice with bok choy and extra soy sauce to taste.

Tips

• Leftover rice works best in stir-fries such as this one.

• Steam the bok choy in a steaming basket over simmering water or blanch in a little boiling water until soft.

Leek and mushroom risotto

Preparation: 10 minutes

Cooking time: 45 minutes

Serves: 4

1 leek, white part only

1 clove garlic

4–6 oz (125–180 g) button mushrooms

6 cups (48 fl oz/1.5 L) chicken stock

2 oz (60 g) butter

2 cups (14 oz/440 g) arborio or short-grain rice

½ cup (2 oz/60 g) grated parmesan

freshly ground black pepper

parmesan shavings, to serve

chopped fresh parsley, to serve

Halve leek lengthwise and rinse under cold running water. Drain and slice thinly. Peel and slice garlic. Halve or quarter mushrooms, if large.

Bring stock to boil in a saucepan over high heat.

Meanwhile, melt butter in a large, heavy-based saucepan over medium heat. Add leek, garlic and mushrooms, and cook stirring, for 3 to 5 minutes, or until leek is soft and liquid from mushrooms has evaporated. Add rice and stir until well coated with butter mixture. Reduce heat and stir in 1 cup (8 fl oz/250 ml) boiling stock. Cook gently, stirring occasionally, until stock is absorbed.

Continue adding stock and cooking in this way for 25 to 30 minutes or until all stock is absorbed and rice is tender but still firm to the bite (al dente).

Stir in grated parmesan and season to taste with pepper. Serve with parmesan shavings and parsley.

Tips

- Add ¼ cup (2 fl oz/60 ml) dry white wine with leeks while they are cooking, and evaporate before adding rice.

- When cooked, risotto should have a creamy consistency; if too stiff, stir in a little extra stock.

- To make parmesan shavings, use a swivel-bladed vegetable peeler to cut thin shavings from a large piece of fresh, room-temperature cheese.

- Serve with a fresh green salad and crusty bread.

Lentils with bacon

Preparation: 10 minutes

Cooking time: 35–40 minutes

Serves: 4–6

3 strips bacon

1 large onion

2 cloves garlic

1 small red bell pepper (capsicum)

1 tablespoon olive oil

1¼ cups (8 oz/250 g) brown or green lentils, rinsed

1 small bay leaf

2 teaspoons chopped fresh sage or thyme or

½ teaspoon dried

freshly ground black pepper

1½–2 cups (12–16 fl oz/375–500 ml) stock or water

2 scallions (spring onions/shallots) with some green
tops

2 sprigs fresh parsley or cilantro (coriander), leaves
only

Remove rind from bacon and discard. Coarsely chop bacon. Peel and chop onion and garlic. Halve bell pepper, remove seeds and cut into ¼-inch (6-mm) pieces.

Heat oil in a large, heavy-based saucepan over medium heat. Add bacon and cook, stirring, for 1 minute. Add onion, garlic and bell pepper and cook for 5 minutes or until onion is golden.

Add lentils, bay leaf, herb and black pepper to taste. Add enough stock to barely cover mixture and bring to boil. Reduce heat, cover and simmer gently for 30 to 40 minutes, or until lentils are tender—not mushy—and liquid has been absorbed.

Thinly slice scallions and chop parsley or cilantro. Sprinkle greens over lentils and serve.

Tips

- Serve with grilled sausages (pictured), chicken or burgers.

- Red or yellow lentils can be used instead of brown or green lentils. They are smaller, however, and so cook more quickly and mush if overcooked. Check after 15 to 20 minutes.

- To make a salad for four people: cook lentils following recipe. While still warm, combine with chopped or sliced salad vegetables—purple onion or scallions (spring onions/shallots), parsley or mint, celery, red bell pepper, unpeeled cucumber—and drizzle with vinaigrette dressing to which garlic and orange rind have been added. Let stand at room temperature for 1 hour before serving to allow flavors to develop.

Middle Eastern burghul pilaf

Preparation: 5 minutes

Cooking time: 20 minutes

Serves: 4

½ cup (4 oz/125 g) butter

1 medium onion, finely chopped

1 clove garlic, minced

1 cup (8 oz/250 g) burghul (bulgur), rinsed and
  drained

1¾ cup (14 fl oz/440 ml) chicken stock

1 tablespoon olive oil

1 lb (500 g) chicken breast fillets

¼ cup (2 fl oz/60 ml) plain (natural) yogurt

2 tablespoons chopped fresh mint

1 tomato, seeded and chopped

1 oz (30 g) sun-dried tomatoes, chopped

Heat butter in frying pan over medium heat. Add onion
and garlic and cook, stirring, for 5 minutes, or until onion
is soft and golden.

Add burghul and stir until well combined. Add enough
stock to pan to cover burghul mixture by 1 inch
(2.5 cm). Bring to a boil, cover pan, reduce heat and
cook until burghul is tender and stock is absorbed,
about 10 minutes.

Meanwhile, heat oil in another frying pan. Add chicken
and cook until lightly browned and tender, about
4 minutes on each side. Let cool. Slice chicken and toss
with yogurt and mint, then serve with burghul and
remaining ingredients (tossed, if desired).

Tips

• Steamed cracked wheat, known as burghul or bulgur,
  makes a simple alternative to the standard rice risotto
  and has a more nutty texture.

• Turkey makes a good substitute for chicken.

• Omit meat and you have a perfect side dish for a stew.

• If the burghul starts to dry out while cooking, add a
  little water to the mixture.

Mixed bean salsa

Preparation: 15 minutes
Serves: 4–6

1 cup (6 oz/180 g) canned garbanzos (chickpeas)
1 cup (6 oz/180 g) canned black eyed beans
1 cup (6 oz/180 g) canned flageolet beans
½ cup (4 oz/180 g) carrots, cut into thin strips
1 small red bell pepper (capsicum) cut into thin
  strips
1 small onion, finely chopped
1 clove garlic, crushed
1 tablespoon cider vinegar
2 tablespoons vegetable oil
½ teaspoon dried tarragon
salt and freshly ground black pepper

Mix the garbanzos, black eyed beans, carrots and bell pepper together in a large bowl.

Mix the onion and garlic with the vinegar, oil, tarragon, salt and pepper. Pour onto the beans and vegetables and mix thoroughly.

Tips

• Any other canned beans could be used, as long as the total weight is kept the same.

• Try replacing one of the canned beans with an equal amount of lightly cooked fresh green beans.

Paella

Preparation: 15 minutes

Cooking time: 40 minutes

Serves: 4

2 chicken quarters (wing or leg)

2 tablespoons olive oil

1 onion, peeled and sliced

1 green bell pepper (capsicum), seeded and sliced

1 red bell pepper (capsicum), seeded and sliced

1–2 cloves garlic, crushed

14 oz (440 g) canned peeled tomatoes

2-inch (5-cm) piece cinnamon bark or stick

salt and pepper

1³⁄₄ cups (15 fl oz/450 ml) chicken stock

¹⁄₄ level teaspoon saffron

2 tablespoons boiling water

1¹⁄₃ cups (7 oz/220 g) long-grain rice

4 oz (125 g) peeled shrimp (prawns), thawed if frozen

4 oz (125 g) squid rings (calamari), thawed if frozen

3 oz (90 g) chorizo (Spanish spiced sausage), sliced

12–16 shrimp (prawns) in shells

6 oz (180 g) frozen peas, thawed

12–16 large fresh mussels, thoroughly cleaned, or
   bottled mussels

Cut the chicken into small pieces, discarding as much of the carcass as possible. Heat the oil in a large frying pan, casserole dish or paella pan and fry the chicken and onion until golden brown.

Add the bell peppers and garlic and continue cooking for 2 to 3 minutes, then add the canned tomatoes and their liquid, cinnamon, seasonings and stock, and bring to a boil. Cover and simmer gently for 15 minutes, until the chicken is tender.

Mix the saffron with the water then add to the pan with the rice and bring back to a boil. Cover and simmer gently for 15 minutes. Stir in the shrimp, squid rings, chorizo, shrimp in shells and peas, and place the mussels on top. Add a little more boiling stock or water if needed. Cover again and simmer for about 10 minutes, or until the rice is tender, all the liquid has been absorbed and the mussel shells have opened. (If any mussels remain closed, discard them.)

Serve paella hot with crusty bread and provide a finger bowl and paper napkins.

Pasta frittata

Preparation: 10 minutes

Cooking time: 20 minutes

Serves: 4

1 tablespoon butter

2 tablespoons olive oil

2 cloves garlic, chopped

1 leek, chopped

2 slices bacon, chopped

4 eggs, lightly beaten

2 tablespoons milk or cream

salt and freshly ground black pepper

½ cup (2 oz/60 g) parmesan, freshly grated

8 oz (250 g) fettuccine, broken in half and cooked
  until just al dente

Melt butter with 1 tablespoon olive oil in a heavy-based frying pan. Add garlic, leek, and bacon and cook until leek is soft, about 5 minutes. Remove from pan; set aside.

Combine eggs, milk, salt, lots of pepper, and half the parmesan in a large bowl. Mix in cooked pasta.

Heat remaining oil over low heat in original pan. Add half the pasta mixture. Top with bacon mixture, then the rest of the pasta mixture. Using a plate, press down firmly to pack tight. Sprinkle remaining parmesan on top.

Cook for 12 minutes to brown bottom, then place under hot broiler (grill) to set and brown top.

Tips

- Serve frittata with Italian tomato sauce and a green salad.

- Try incorporating any chopped vegetables you have on hand—tomato, mushrooms, bell peppers (capsicum), zucchini (courgette), or arugula (rocket)—instead of, or with, the leek at the start.

- Substitute ham, salami, pancetta, or leftover cooked meat for the bacon.

- Herbs make a welcome addition, fresh or dried. Try basil, oregano, or thyme.

- Add a handful of shredded mozzarella with the parmesan if you like it cheesier. This will also help it to hold together.

Pasta with spiced, baked meatballs

Preparation: 15 minutes

Cooking time: 15 minutes

Serves: 2

10 oz (300 g) ground (minced) beef

¼ cup (1½ oz/50 g) fine dry breadcrumbs

2 tablespoons finely chopped pitted (stoned) olives

1 clove garlic, pressed (crushed)

¼ teaspoon ground coriander

¼ teaspoon ground cumin

1 tablespoon chopped fresh parsley

1 teaspoon finely grated lemon zest

salt and freshly ground pepper

8 oz (250 g) pasta

2½ cups (20 fl oz/625 ml) store-bought tomato sauce

2 tablespoons finely grated parmesan, to serve

chopped fresh basil, to serve

Heat oven to 350°F (180°C/Gas 4). Combine meat, breadcrumbs, olives, garlic, spices, parsley, lemon zest and salt and pepper in bowl.

Form into ½-inch (2-cm) meatballs. Place on baking sheet and bake for 10 to 15 minutes.

Meanwhile, cook pasta in large saucepan of boiling salted water until al dente. Drain. Warm the tomato sauce.

Serve meatballs over hot pasta with tomato sauce. Sprinkle with parmesan and basil.

Tip

For tastier meatballs, use a combination of 5 oz (150 g) each ground (minced) beef and veal or pork.

Pasta with tomato sauce

Preparation: 10–15 minutes

Cooking time: 10–12 minutes

Serves: 4

2½ lb (1.25 kg) ripe tomatoes

1 clove garlic

2 tablespoons olive oil

2–3 tablespoons chopped fresh basil leaves or
  2 teaspoons dried

1 lb (500 g) pasta, cooked, to serve

chopped fresh basil, to serve

parmesan shavings, to serve

Rinse tomatoes and place 2 or 3 at a time in a saucepan of simmering water for 30 to 45 seconds, or until skins begin to break. Remove with a slotted spoon and drain.

Use a sharp knife to peel off skins and remove cores; discard. Place tomatoes, in batches, in a blender or food processor and process briefly into coarse chunks.

Peel and slice garlic. Heat oil in a large, heavy-based saucepan over medium heat. Add garlic and sauté 1 minute. Add tomatoes and basil and bring to a boil, stirring constantly. Reduce heat and simmer for 8 to 10 minutes, or until sauce thickens. Serve with hot cooked pasta, sprinkled with basil and parmesan if desired (pictured).

Tips

• When fully ripe tomatoes are unavailable, use 2 x 14 oz (400 g) cans whole, peeled, undrained tomatoes. Crush tomatoes or place in a food processor and blend briefly.

• For variety, add 2 to 3 slices chopped bacon or prosciutto, 6 to 8 sliced stuffed green olives or 1 teaspoon chopped hot red chili or dried chili flakes to pan when sautéing garlic.

Pumpkin, ricotta and pesto pasta

Preparation: 10 minutes

Cooking time: 15 minutes

Serves: 2

2 cups (4 oz/125 g) chopped fresh basil

1 clove garlic

¼ cup (2 fl oz/60 ml) light olive oil

¼ cup (1 oz/30 g) finely grated parmesan

1 tablespoon pine nuts, toasted

14 oz (440 g) peeled pumpkin, cut into 1-inch
  (2.5-cm) cubes

1 tablespoon butter

2 tablespoons light (single) cream or warm water

salt and freshly ground pepper

8 oz (250 g) fresh pasta

5 oz (150 g) ricotta cheese, in one piece

1 teaspoon olive oil

To make pesto, blend basil with garlic in food processor until leaves are coarsely chopped. With motor running, add olive oil in steady stream. Add parmesan and pine nuts and process until combined and almost smooth.

Steam or boil pumpkin until tender. Mash, adding butter, cream, salt and pepper. Keep warm.

Meanwhile, put pasta on to boil.

Cut ricotta into slices ½ inch (1 cm) thick and arrange on baking sheet. Brush with a little olive oil and broil (grill) at medium heat for 3 minutes on each side. Remove and crumble.

Drain pasta. Stir pumpkin through cooked pasta and serve immediately topped with crumbled ricotta and pesto.

Tip

You can make your own pesto or use a prepared variety. This recipe makes about 1 cup (8 fl oz/250 ml), which can be stored in the refrigerator for up to 1 week.

Rice fritters

Preparation: 15 minutes

Cooking time: 15 minutes

Serves: 4–5 (makes about 16 fritters)

1 cup (4 oz/125 g) all-purpose (plain) flour

salt and pepper

2 eggs

1 cup (8 fl oz/250 ml) milk

1¼ cups (6 oz/180 g) cooked rice (long grain, Basmati, brown etc.)

4 oz (125 g) cooked peas

7 oz (220 g) canned corn kernels, drained

2 level tablespoons snipped chives or green (spring) onion tops

vegetable oil or shortening (lard) for frying

2 level tablespoons freshly grated parmesan

6 tablespoons (3 oz/90 g) fromage frais

2 level tablespoons snipped chives

1 tablespoon wine vinegar

Sift the flour into a bowl and season well with salt and pepper. Make a well in the middle and add the eggs and half the milk. Whisk until smooth and then slowly add the rest of the milk and continue to whisk until smooth. Add the cooked rice, peas, corn and chives.

Heat a little oil or shortening in a frying pan and add heaped tablespoons of the mixture. Cook for 2 to 3 minutes, until golden brown underneath, then turn over carefully and cook the other side.

Meanwhile, combine the fromage frais, chives and wine vinegar, and mix well to make a sauce.

When fritters are golden brown, drain on paper towel; put onto a plate and sprinkle each lightly with grated parmesan. Serve warm with sauce.

Tips

• Add diced cooked bacon, ham or poultry to the fritter.

• Make smaller fritters and serve cold as a snack.

Rigatoni with roasted eggplant

Preparation: 10 minutes

Cooking time: 15 minutes

Serves: 4

1 large eggplant (aubergine)

salt

about 2 tablespoons olive oil

1–2 cloves garlic, chopped

1 lb (500 g) rigatoni

1 cup (8 fl oz/250 ml) Italian tomato sauce or pasta
  sauce

3½ oz (100 g) goat cheese, to serve

Cut eggplant lengthwise into thin slices. Sprinkle liberally
with salt and let stand for a few minutes to disgorge
juices. Pat dry with paper towel.

Place eggplant slices on tray under broiler (grill), brush
with about 1 tablespoon olive oil and sprinkle with garlic.
Cook under high heat until very brown, about 15 minutes,
turning to cook both sides and brushing occasionally with
more olive oil.

Meanwhile, boil pasta until al dente. Drain; return to hot
saucepan with tomato sauce and toss.

Cut eggplant into strips and toss through pasta with
crumbled goat cheese.

Tips

• You can use store-bought tomato sauce or make your
  own.

• Add a spoonful of homemade or store-bought pesto or
  tapenade if desired.

• Try shavings of parmesan or cubes of feta instead of
  goat cheese. Or top each serving with a large spoonful
  of ricotta.

Sardines and anchovy spaghetti

Preparation: 5 minutes

Cooking time: 15 minutes

Serves: 4

2 tablespoons olive oil

2 cloves garlic, minced

7 oz (220 g) canned sardines in oil, drained

4 canned or bottled anchovy fillets

5 very ripe tomatoes, finely chopped

1 tablespoon tomato paste

grated zest and juice of 1 lemon

1/4 cup (2 oz/60 g) finely chopped fresh cilantro
  (coriander) leaves or parsley

1 lb (500 g) spaghetti, cooked and drained

Heat oil in large saucepan over low heat. Add garlic and cook until fragrant and lightly golden. Stir in sardines and anchovies and cook until soft and easy to mash with the back of a spoon.

Mash the fish, then add tomatoes, tomato paste, lemon zest and juice. Cook, stirring, until heated through and well combined, about 10 minutes.

Toss hot cooked spaghetti with fish sauce and fresh coriander. Serve immediately.

Tip

The fresh tomatoes and tomato paste can be replaced by 14 oz (440 g) canned tomatoes.

Spaghetti carbonara

Preparation: 5 minutes

Cooking time: 15 minutes

Serves: 4

1lb (500 g) spaghetti

5 tablespoons extra virgin olive oil

2 large cloves garlic, finely chopped

4 red chilies, seeded and sliced (optional)

4 oz (125 g) bacon or pancetta, chopped

2 eggs, lightly beaten

½ cup (2 oz/60 g) parmesan, freshly grated

freshly ground black pepper

Cook pasta until al dente, usually 5 to 12 minutes. Meanwhile, add oil, garlic, chili, and bacon to a large frying pan and cook over low heat for a few minutes, until garlic is pale golden and bacon has cooked.

Drain pasta; add immediately to frying pan. Take pan off heat and immediately add eggs and parmesan. Toss through, allowing the heat of the pasta to "cook" the eggs and parmesan.

Grind loads of pepper over the pasta and serve immediately.

Tips

• For a thinner but richer sauce, use egg yolks only. Beat 4 yolks with a couple of tablespoons of single (light) cream.

• Use thin strips of ham or prosciutto instead of bacon.

• Add chopped onion with the garlic.

• Add sliced mushrooms instead of, or along with, the bacon. You could add 1 cup peas too.

• Blanched fresh asparagus or a drained can of asparagus is a good addition. Add to the frying pan after the bacon has cooked and toss to warm through.

• Pecorino romano is a good substitute for parmesan.

Spaghetti with roasted pepper and anchovy sauce

Preparation: 10–35 minutes

Cooking time: 15 minutes

Serves: 2

8 oz (250 g) spaghetti

⅓ cup (3 fl oz/90 ml) virgin olive oil

3 tablespoons finely chopped canned anchovies

2 cloves garlic, minced

2 tablespoons finely chopped fresh parsley

1 red bell pepper (capsicum), roasted, seeded,
   peeled and cut into strips

freshly ground pepper

2 tablespoons finely grated parmesan

finely chopped lemon zest, to serve

chopped fresh basil or parsley, to serve

Cook spaghetti in large saucepan of boiling salted water until al dente. Drain.

Meanwhile, warm olive oil in frying pan. Add anchovies and cook over low heat until anchovies have dissolved and combined with oil.

Add garlic and cook over medium heat for 1 minute. Add parsley, roasted bell pepper and ground pepper and cook for 1 minute.

Stir sauce through hot spaghetti. Serve with parmesan, lemon zest and chopped herbs.

Tips

• Serve pasta with pieces of warmed Italian bread, with lemon wedges on the side.

• To roast peppers: There are a number of methods. You can place a whole pepper directly on an oven rack and bake in a preheated 450°F (230°C/Gas 8) oven for about 20 to 30 minutes, or use a cooking fork to hold the pepper over a gas flame for 5 to 10 minutes. Alternatively, the pepper can be cooked whole or halved under a hot broiler (grill) for 5 to 15 minutes. Peppers are done when the skin is blackened and blistered; whole peppers should be turned frequently during cooking. Peel off skin—do not rinse. Remove core, seeds and membrane.

Spiced couscous with fruit and nuts

Preparation: 5 minutes

Cooking time: 5 minutes

Serves: 4

½ cup (2½ oz/75 g) pine nuts

2 cups (12 oz/375 g) couscous

1½ cups (12 fl oz/375 ml) boiling water

large pinch salt

1 tablespoon butter

1 onion, finely chopped

½ teaspoon ground cinnamon

¼ cup (1½ oz/45 g) currants or raisins

½ cup (9 oz/280 g) dried apricots, chopped

3 tablespoons extra butter, in pieces

Toast pine nuts in a dry heavy-based frying pan. Set aside.

Place couscous in a large bowl, pour in boiling water and stir in salt. Let stand about 3 to 5 minutes, until water is absorbed.

Meanwhile, melt 1 tablespoon butter in frying pan. Add onion and fry until soft Stir in cinnamon, dried fruit, and pine nuts.

Mix pieces of butter through warm couscous with a fork to fluff it up. Add onion spice mixture, stir through and serve.

Tips

• To make this a heartier meal, you could add 8 oz (250 g) lean ground (minced) beef or sliced lamb or chicken. Fry the meat with the onion.

• Instead of meat—or along with it—add slices of zucchini (courgette) and carrot, strips of red pepper (capsicum), cubes of eggplant (aubergine), or a cup of canned chick peas (garbanzo beans).

• Try a teaspoon of cumin and/or ground coriander instead of the cinnamon.

• Add chopped walnuts or sliced almonds instead of pine nuts.

• If you have time, soak the dried fruit in water to cover for an hour so they plump up.

Spiced lentils

Preparation: 5 minutes

Cooking time: 10 minutes

Serves: 2–4

3 tablespoons vegetable oil

1 clove garlic, chopped

1 onion, chopped

1 teaspoon cumin

1/4 teaspoon turmeric

1 teaspoon ground cilantro (coriander)

1/4 teaspoon cayenne pepper, or to taste

3 large tomatoes, or 14 oz (440 g) can tomatoes, chopped

1 teaspoon minced ginger

2 x 13 oz (400 g/about 4 cups) canned lentils, undrained

squeeze lemon juice (optional)

aioli, to serve

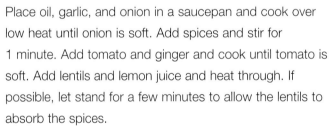

Place oil, garlic, and onion in a saucepan and cook over low heat until onion is soft. Add spices and stir for 1 minute. Add tomato and ginger and cook until tomato is soft. Add lentils and lemon juice and heat through. If possible, let stand for a few minutes to allow the lentils to absorb the spices.

Serve with a dollop of aioli.

Tomato and tuna pasta

Preparation: 5 minutes

Cooking time: 10 minutes

Serves: 4

1 lb (500 g) pasta shells, cooked and drained

1 tablespoon olive oil

1 medium onion, chopped

6 oz (180 g) canned tuna (water-packed), drained

2 tablespoons white wine

1 can (14 oz/440 g) chopped tomatoes, undrained

¾ cup (6 fl oz/180 ml) half-and-half or light cream

3 oz (90 g) pitted (stoned) black olives

2 tablespoons prepared pesto

Cook pasta in boiling salted water until al dente.

Meanwhile, heat oil in saucepan over medium heat. Add onion and cook, stirring, until soft. Add tuna, wine, tomatoes and cream and cook over medium heat, stirring occasionally, for 5 minutes or until heated through. Add olives and pesto and heat through, stirring.

Serve over drained, cooked pasta.

Tips

- Other canned fish, such as salmon or sardines, can be substituted for tuna.

- The pesto can also be replaced by 2 cloves of minced garlic and a tablespoon of dried herbs.

- Any pasta can be used, fresh or dried.

Warm lentil salad

Preparation: 10 minutes
Cooking time: 10 minutes
Serves: 2

2 teaspoons olive oil
2 teaspoons butter
1 small carrot, chopped
1 celery stalk, chopped
1 small onion, chopped
1 can (14 oz/440 g) lentils, drained
¼ cup (2 fl oz/60 ml) chicken stock
1 tablespoon chopped fresh parsley
10 oz (300 g) lamb fillets
¼ cup (2 fl oz/60 ml) sour cream or crème fraîche
1 tablespoon prepared horseradish
flat-leaf parsley, to serve

Heat oil and butter in saucepan. Add carrot, celery and onion and cook over medium heat, partially covered, for 5 minutes. Add lentils and stock and bring to boil. Simmer for 2 to 3 minutes. Stir in parsley.

Meanwhile, grill or broil lamb at medium heat until cooked through, 3 to 4 minutes on each side.

Combine sour cream and horseradish. Serve with meat and lentils, garnished with parsley.

Tips

• Serve lentils with chicken or salmon instead of lamb. Grill or broil 2 chicken breasts (about 14 oz/440 g) for 5 minutes each side, or 14 oz (420 g) salmon steaks for 3 minutes each side.

• You can substitute another canned bean, such as haricots or cannellini.

Wild mushroom and parmesan fettuccine

Preparation: 5 minutes
Cooking time: 20 minutes
Serves: 4

2 tablespoons olive oil
1 medium onion, finely chopped
3 cloves garlic, minced
14 oz (440 g) wild mushrooms
1 lb (500 g) fettuccine
3 oz (90 g) parmesan, finely grated
1½ cups (12 fl oz/375 ml) half-and-half or light cream
3 tablespoons chopped fresh chives
shaved parmesan, to serve

Heat oil in large frying pan over medium heat. Add onion and garlic and cook, stirring, until onion is soft. Add mushrooms and cook, stirring, until just tender, about 3 minutes.

Meanwhile, cook fettuccine in large pot of boiling salted water. Add grated parmesan and cream to mushrooms in frying pan and cook, stirring occasionally, for 10 minutes or until mixture has thickened slightly.

Stir in chives and drained fettuccine. Serve sprinkled with shaved parmesan.

Tips

- Any seasonal wild mushrooms can be used, but avoid using regular button mushrooms, as they don't have as much flavor.

- Parmigiano reggiano is the ultimate Italian parmesan cheese and is highly recommended for this dish, but any full-flavored parmesan will do.

- The sauce mixes well with fettuccine, but penne, thick spaghetti or linguine make an adequate alternative.

seafood

THE HENLEY COLLEGE LIBRARY

Baked fish with rice stuffing

Preparation: 10 minutes

Cooking time: 50 minutes

Serves: 4

1 cup (7 oz/220 g) white rice

½ teaspoon ground turmeric

¼ cup (1 oz/30 g) roughly chopped almonds or
  hazelnuts

2–3 tablespoons chopped parsley

2–3 teaspoons grated lemon rind

1 egg, lightly beaten

4 x 5–6 oz (150–180 g) whole fish (e.g. trout, bream,
  snapper), cleaned and scaled

freshly ground black pepper

1 oz (30 g) butter, melted

¼ cup (2 fl oz/60 ml) lemon juice

For stuffing, boil rice using rapid boil method, adding turmeric to water. Drain and let cool.

Roast nuts in a dry, nonstick frying pan over medium heat, stirring occasionally until brown. Remove from pan immediately to prevent overbrowning.

Combine rice and nuts in a bowl with parsley, lemon rind and egg, using a fork.

Preheat oven to 350°F (180°C/Gas 4). Rinse fish, inside and out, under cold running water and dry with paper towel. Sprinkle cavities lightly with black pepper and loosely fill with stuffing. Place fish, in one layer, in baking dish. Drizzle with melted butter and lemon juice.

Cover dish and bake for 35 to 40 minutes, or until fish flakes easily from backbone when pierced with the tip of a knife.

Tips

• Most fish, whether white-fleshed or oily, whole or in fillets or steaks (cutlets), can be baked conventionally or microwaved. Whole trout are pictured.

• You can use thick fillets or steaks (cutlets) in this recipe—place the rice mixture in a baking dish, cover with a single layer of fish fillets and cook as directed.

• To microwave: arrange fish in one layer in a shallow, microwavable dish, with thickest parts pointing to the outside. If whole fish is thick, slash skin in 2 or 3 places with a sharp knife. Remove or pierce eyes as they can explode. Drizzle with melted butter and lemon juice. Cover and cook on medium–high (70% power) for 5 to 6 minutes per 1 lb (500 g) or until fish flakes easily. If using thicker fillets or steaks, cook on high (100% power) for 4 to 5 minutes per 1 lb (500 g). The secret to perfectly microwaved fish is to bring it to the table still cooking! Undercook fish slightly so that by the time it's served, the fish is just cooked and still quite moist.

• For a slightly sweet finish to the stuffing, add a touch of curry powder or curry paste and some chopped seedless raisins or dried apricots.

Baked Greek-style fish

Preparation: 5 minutes

Cooking time: 10 minutes

Serves: 4

4 fish fillets

4 teaspoons olive oil

2 medium tomatoes, sliced

½ cup pitted (stoned) black olives, roughly chopped

2 tablespoon parsley, chopped

1 tablespoon fresh oregano, chopped, or 2 teaspoons dried

2 cloves garlic, crushed

4 teaspoons lemon rind, grated

4 teaspoons lemon juice

Preheat oven to 350°F (180°C/Gas 4).

For each parcel, you will need a piece of greased foil, big enough to wrap fish and ingredients.

Divide ingredients equally among the four parcels. Place fish on the middle of the foil sheet. Spread fish with oil then top with tomatoes. Sprinkle remaining ingredients over.

Fold the two longest (opposite) sides of foil so that they meet in the middle. Fold this edge over and over so that it will be tightly sealed. Fold up the other ends of parcel.

Place parcel on baking sheet with the folded edges up so that the juices do not run out. Bake in oven for about 10 minutes, depending on thickness. Thicker pieces may take longer to cook.

Remove fish from foil and serve with couscous or baby (new) potatoes.

Barbecued shrimp with pecorino polenta

Preparation: 15 minutes

Cooking time: 40 minutes

Serves: 4

1 cup (6 oz/180 g) polenta

1 teaspoon salt

1 cup (8 fl oz/250 ml) cold water

2 cups (16 fl oz/500 ml) boiling water or fish stock

¼ cup (1 oz/30 g) grated pecorino cheese

olive oil, for cooking

1½ lb (750 g) uncooked jumbo shrimp (large
   prawns), peeled and deveined

small bunch arugula (rocket), trimmed and washed

4 plum (egg) tomatoes, quartered

⅓ cup (3 fl oz/90 ml) extra virgin olive oil

2 tablespoons balsamic vinegar

3 tablespoons chopped fresh basil

3 cloves garlic, chopped

freshly ground pepper, to serve

Combine polenta, salt and cold water in a saucepan and mix well. Pour in boiling water or stock and bring to a boil. Cook over medium heat for 10 minutes, stirring constantly. Cover and continue to cook, over very low heat, for 15 minutes. Stir in pecorino. Pour into sn oiled 8-in x 8-inch (20-cm x 20-cm) square cake tin and let cool.

Using a sharp knife, cut polenta into 3-inch (7-cm) squares. Brush with oil and broil (grill) until golden and toasted.

Preheat barbecue or broiler (grill) and brush with oil to prevent sticking. Brush shrimp with oil and cook for 1 to 2 minutes per side, or until tender.

To serve, place polenta squares on plates. Top with some arugula, then shrimp and tomato. Combine extra virgin olive oil, vinegar, basil, and garlic and drizzle over. Grind pepper over the shrimp and serve.

Battered fried fish

Preparation: 10 minutes
Cooking time: 10–15 minutes
Serves: 4

1 egg
1 cup (8 fl oz/250 ml) chilled mineral water or club
    soda (soda water)
1 cup (4 oz/125 g) all-purpose (plain) flour
1½ lb (750 g) boneless, skinned fish fillets (e.g.
bream, snapper, dory, perch, cod)
vegetable or peanut oil, for deep frying
lemon wedges and parsley sprigs, to serve
brown vinegar, to serve

To make batter, place egg and water in a bowl and, using a whisk, stir to combine. Sift flour into egg mixture and whisk lightly until just blended (batter should be slightly lumpy).

Set oven temperature to 300°F (150°C/Gas 2). Cut fish into thick strips and pat thoroughly dry with paper towel. Line a baking sheet with paper towel.

Pour oil into a large, heavy-based saucepan to a depth of 4 inches (10 cm) and heat slowly to 350°F (180°C). Use a candy thermometer if you have one or test oil by frying a cube of bread in the oil—it should brown in 20 to 30 seconds.

Using tongs, dip fish pieces, three at a time, into batter. Gently drain off excess. Carefully lower into hot oil and deep-fry in batches, turning once, for 3 to 5 minutes, or until golden brown and crisp. Use a slotted spoon to lift out cooked pieces. Drain in a single layer on lined baking sheet.

Keep fish warm in oven while frying remaining pieces. Scoop out any floating pieces of batter from oil between batches.

Serve with lemon, parsley and vinegar as desired.

Tips

• Can be served with oven-baked potato wedges and tartare sauce.

• To prevent boiling over, never fill a saucepan with oil more than half-full, and never use a lid when deep-frying.

• For best results, cook foods in small batches so as not to crowd the pan. Allow the oil to return to cooking temperature between each batch. If the oil begins to smoke, the temperature is too high.

Calamari rings

Preparation: 10 minutes plus 30 minutes chilling

Cooking time: 2–20 minutes

Serves: 4

2 lb (1 kg) squid (calamari), cleaned and cut into
   rings

seasoned all-purpose (plain) flour

2 eggs, beaten

1½ cups (6 oz/180 g) dry breadcrumbs

oil for deep frying

tartare sauce, to serve

lemon wedges, to serve

Dust squid with flour, shaking off excess. Dip into egg
and then breadcrumbs, pressing firmly. Chill for
30 minutes.

Heat oil in deep pan over medium heat until hot. Add
squid in batches and cook until crisp and golden, about
1 to 2 minutes each batch. Drain well on paper towel
and keep warm. Serve with tartare sauce and lemon
wedges.

Tip

To make calamari rings crisp and golden, the oil must be
at the correct temperature. To test, sprinkle a few
breadcrumbs into the hot oil; they should start to sizzle
immediately but not burn. Do not overcrowd the pan
with squid as this will lower the temperature of the oil
and give soggy results.

Continental fish cakes

Preparation: 15 minutes

Cooking time: 10 minutes

Serves: 4

1¼ lb (625 g) cod, ling or haddock

1 small onion, finely chopped

1 clove garlic, crushed

½ oz (15 g) low-fat polyunsaturated margarine

2 oz (60 g) crackers, crushed

8 oz (250 g) zucchini (courgettes), ends removed and
   grated

2 tablespoons chopped parsley

1 tablespoon lemon juice

few drops Tabasco sauce

1 egg, beaten

salt and freshly ground black pepper

¼ cup (1 oz/30 g) all-purpose (plain) flour

1 tablespoon sunflower oil

lemon wedges and parsley sprigs, to serve

Put fish into pan of cold water, bring to a boil, then simmer for 5 minutes. Drain well then flake into a bowl, removing any skin and bones.

Cook the onion and garlic in margarine until soft, then add to the fish with the crackers, zucchini, parsley, lemon juice, Tabasco and egg. Season with salt and pepper. Mix well and form into eight even-sized patties. Coat patties in flour.

Heat the oil in a large non-stick frying pan and cook each fish cake for 4 to 5 minutes each side. Drain well on paper towel. Serve garnished with lemon and parsley.

Dill and lime fishburgers

Preparation: 15 minutes
Cooking time: 10 minutes
Serves: 2

¼ cup (2 fl oz/60 ml) mayonnaise
¼ cup (2 fl oz/60 ml) sour cream
2 teaspoons drained capers
about 7 oz (220 g) boneless fish fillets, such as perch
3 scallions (spring onions/shallots), chopped
1 tablespoon chopped fresh dill
2 teaspoons finely grated lime zest
1 tablespoon lime juice
salt and freshly ground pepper
1 egg, beaten
vegetable oil, for cooking

To make dressing, combine mayonnaise, sour cream and capers. Refrigerate until ready to serve.

Process fish in processor until almost smooth. Stir in scallions, dill, lime zest and juice, salt, pepper and egg. Form into four patties ½ inch (1.5 cm) thick.

Heat oil in frying pan and cook patties for 2 to 3 minutes each side. Serve hot with dressing.

Tips

• Serve the patties inside soft rolls with a crisp salad of tomato, avocado, lettuce and this special dressing (pictured). Provide additional wedges of lime, if desired.

• Using a nonstick pan makes cooking easier.

Fish stew

Preparation: 10–15 minutes

Cooking time: 35–40 minutes

Serves: 6

1 small leek

1 onion

2 cloves garlic

2 tablespoon olive oil

14 oz (400 g) can whole, peeled tomatoes

3 cups (24 fl oz/750 ml) fish stock or water

2 tablespoons each chopped fresh basil and parsley
  or 1½ teaspoons dried

1 tablespoon chopped fresh thyme or 1 teaspoon
  dried

1 bay leaf

2–3 drops hot pepper sauce, such as Tabasco

2 lb (1 kg) boneless, skinned, white-fleshed fish
  fillets (e.g. bream, snapper, ling, cod)

freshly ground black pepper

parsley sprigs, to serve

Remove green part of leek, halve white part lengthwise. Wash clean under cold running water, drain and slice thinly crosswise. Peel and thinly slice onion. Peel and finely chop garlic.

Heat oil in a large, heavy-based saucepan. Cook leek, onion and garlic over medium heat, stirring, for 5 minutes, or until golden.

Crush tomatoes and add with their juice to pan. Add stock, herbs, and hot pepper sauce. Bring to a boil, reduce heat and simmer for 25 to 30 minutes.

Cut fish into large, bite-size pieces, add to pan and simmer for 5 to 10 minutes, or until tender. Season to taste with black pepper.

Ladle fish and stock into wide, deep soup plates. Serve garnished with parsley.

Tips

• Any combination of firm white-fleshed (non-oily) fish can be used to make a simple soup-stew. Serve with a good white wine and crusty bread.

• For the look and taste of the French fish soup known as bouillabaisse, replace ¾ cup (6 fl oz/180 ml) of the stock or water in this recipe with dry white wine and add 2 to 3 thin strips of orange rind (scraping off all white pith) and a pinch of saffron powder or ground turmeric when you add stock.z

Gingered fish fillets with coriander rice

Preparation: 5 minutes

Cooking time: 25 minutes

Serves: 4

1½ lbs (750 g) firm-fleshed oily fish fillets

3 tablespoons vegetable oil

1 small onion, finely chopped

6 scallions (spring onions/shallots), sliced

1 tablespoon grated fresh ginger

¼ cup (2 fl oz/60 ml) soy sauce

2 teaspoons brown sugar

½ cup (4 fl oz/125 ml) fish stock

2 cups (13 oz/400 g) long-grain rice

3½ cups (28 fl oz/825 ml) water

2 tablespoons chopped fresh cilantro (coriander)
  leaves

Rinse rice in strainer under cold water until water runs clear. Combine rice and 3½ cups water in a heavy-based saucepan and bring to boil, stirring. Reduce heat, cover tightly and simmer gently for 12 minutes. Remove from heat and let stand, covered, for 10 minutes. Fluff rice with a fork, stirring in coriander.

Meanwhile, cut fish into large pieces. Heat oil in a large frying pan over medium-high heat. Add fish and cook, turning occasionally, until lightly browned on all sides. Remove from pan.

Add onion and scallions to pan and cook, stirring, for 1 minute. Add ginger, soy sauce, sugar and stock and bring to a boil. Return fish to pan, cover and simmer for 5 minutes. Remove pan from heat.

Serve rice topped with fish pieces and drizzled with sauce.

Lobster quenelles with red pepper coulis

Preparation: 15 minutes plus possible 15 minutes
  chilling
Cooking time: 15 minutes
Serves: 4

2 red bell peppers (capsicums)
¼ cup (2 fl oz/60 ml) extra virgin olive oil
freshly ground pepper
1 lb (500 g) uncooked lobster tail
1 cup (8 fl oz/250 ml) single (light) cream
1 egg white
½ teaspoon salt
2 tablespoons chopped chives

Broil (grill) bell peppers until skin blisters and blackens. Let cool then peel away skin and remove seeds. Place peppers in a food processor and puree until smooth. Add oil and pepper and mix well. Set aside.

Extract meat from lobster tail and cut into small pieces. Place in food processor and puree until smooth. With motor running, gradually add cream, egg white, salt and chives and blend well. Mixture should be firm enough to mold; if not, chill for 15 minutes.

Pour about 1 inch (2.5 cm) water into frying pan and bring to a boil. Turn down to simmer. Using wetted tablespoons, mold quenelle mixture into egg shapes and drop into water. Simmer for 1 to 2 minutes per side. Do not allow water to boil or quenelles will fall apart. Drain quenelles on paper towels and serve with a small amount of the red pepper coulis at room temperature.

Tip
Shrimp (prawns), crayfish and white-fleshed fish fillets make good substitutes for the lobster. You will need about 8 oz (250 g), not including shell weight.

Mackerel stuffed with orange and olives

Preparation: 20 minutes

Cooking time: 35 minutes

Serves: 4

2 oranges

1 small onion, chopped

½ oz (15 g) low-fat polyunsaturated margarine

¾ cup (3 oz/90 g) fresh wholewheat breadcrumbs

½ cup (2 oz/60 g) pitted (stoned) green olives, chopped

1½ teaspoons dried tarragon

salt and freshly ground black pepper

1 small egg, beaten

4 mackerel, heads removed, cleaned and boned

½ cup (4 fl oz/125 ml) water

1 orange, sliced, to serve

sprigs fresh tarragon, to serve

Preheat oven to 375°F (190°C, Gas 5).

Grate peel from oranges then peel fully; remove all white pith. Divide orange into segments then cut each segment in half. Reserve any juice.

Cook onion in margarine until soft. Add breadcrumbs, orange peel and segments, olives, tarragon, salt and pepper. Bind mixture together with beaten egg.

Lay mackerel flat, skin side down. Put one quarter of the stuffing at head end of each one. Roll up the fish from head end and secure filling with wooden toothpicks (cocktail sticks).

Place mackerel in a shallow ovenproof dish. Pour in the water and any reserved orange juice. Cover with foil and cook in oven for 30 to 35 minutes.

Remove toothpicks before serving and garnish with orange slices and tarragon sprigs.

Mussels steamed in wine

Preparation: 5 minutes

Cooking time: 15 minutes

Serves: 4–6

1 tablespoon olive oil

2 cloves garlic, chopped

½ cup (4 fl oz/125 ml) dry white wine

½ cup (4 fl oz/125 ml) fish stock

2 scallions (spring onions/shallots), chopped

3 tablespoons chopped fresh parsley

2 lb (1 kg) mussels, scrubbed and debearded

crusty bread, to serve

Heat oil in large saucepan over medium heat. Add garlic and sauté until fragrant. Add wine, stock, scallions, parsley, and mussels. Cover and bring to a boil. Simmer just until mussels open, about 2 to 3 minutes. Discard any mussels that do not open. Serve immediately with bread.

Old English fish pie

Preparation: 25 minutes

Cooking time: 25 minutes

Serves: 4

1½ lb (750 g) potatoes, peeled

salt

1 oz (30 g) low-fat polyunsaturated margarine

1½ cups (12 fl oz/375 ml) low-fat (skimmed) milk

12 oz (375 g) smoked fish (haddock, cod or ling)

8 oz (250 g) fresh fish (haddock, cod or ling)

1 bay leaf

1 blade mace

6 black peppercorns

1 tablespoon cornstarch (cornflour)

3 tablespoons chopped parsley

2 hard-cooked (boiled) eggs, chopped

¼ cup (1 oz/30 g) low-fat sharp (mature) cheese

Preheat oven to 400°F (200°C/Gas 6).

Cook the potatoes in lightly salted water for about 20 minutes, until soft. Drain well then mash with the margarine and 3 tablespoons milk.

Put fish into a pan with the remaining milk, bay leaf, mace and peppercorns. Bring to a boil, simmer for 2 to 3 minutes, then remove from heat. Cover pan and let stand until fish is cool enough to handle.

Strain milk into another pan, discarding the bay leaf, mace and peppercorns. Mix the cornstarch with a little cold water and add to the milk. Bring to a boil, stirring continuously. Simmer for 2 to 3 minutes.

Flake the fish, removing any skin and bones. Add fish to the sauce with the parsley and eggs. Taste and adjust seasoning. Transfer the mixture to a deep ovenproof dish, top with the mashed potatoes, running the prongs of a fork down the length of the potatoes. Sprinkle with grated cheese.

Cook in the preheated oven for about 25 minutes, until topping is browned.

Tip

This pie can be cooked in a microwave. Cover with microwave-safe plastic wrap pierced in a few places and microwave on medium for 12 to 15 minutes, finishing off under the broiler (grill) to brown the top.

Panfried dory with slivered almonds and snow peas

Preparation: 5 minutes

Cooking time: 15 minutes

Serves: 4

6 tablespoons butter

1 lb (500 g) Dory or similar white-fleshed or oily fish fillet

½ cup (1½ oz/45 g) slivered almonds

⅓ cup (½ oz/15 oz) chopped scallions (shallots/spring onions)

7 oz/220 g snow peas (mange-tout), steamed

2 tablespoons dry white wine

salt and freshly ground pepper

Melt 2 tablespoons butter in frying pan over medium heat. Add fish and cook for 2 to 3 minutes per side, or until fish is opaque and beginning to flake when tested. Remove and keep warm.

Add almonds to pan juices and cook over medium heat until golden, about 1 to 2 minutes. Stir in remaining butter, scallions, snow peas, wine, and salt and pepper. Stir until sauce boils and thickens slightly.

To serve, place fillets on plates and pour sauce over.

Panfried fish fillets with lemon, garlic, capers and parsley

Preparation: 5 minutes

Cooking time: 10 minutes

Serves: 2

1 tablespoon butter

1 teaspoon olive oil

2 firm, thick white-fleshed fish fillets, such as
snapper (about 14 oz/440 g)

2 teaspoons grated lemon zest

juice of ½ lemon

1 clove garlic, minced

2 teaspoons drained capers

1 tablespoon chopped fresh parsley

salt and freshly ground pepper

Melt butter with oil in frying pan over medium heat. Add fillets and cook for 2 to 3 minutes on first side.

Turn fish and sprinkle with remaining ingredients. Cook for 3 minutes, or until just opaque.

Serve immediately.

Tips

• Simple accompaniments are all that's needed—steamed or baked new potatoes and green salad or steamed spinach.

• To make crisp baked potatoes for two, you will need 14 oz (440 g) new potatoes, 1 tablespoon olive oil and salt to taste. Preheat oven to 400°F (200°C/Gas 6). Halve potatoes and brush cut sides with oil. Arrange on baking sheet, cut side up. Sprinkle with salt and bake until crisp and golden, about 30 minutes.

Parmesan-crusted fish with tomato and basil salad

Preparation: 15 minutes

Cooking time: 20 minutes

Serves: 2

3/4 cup (1 1/2 oz/45 g) fresh breadcrumbs

1 tablespoon cold butter

2 tablespoons grated parmesan

2 teaspoons toasted pine nuts

1 anchovy fillet (optional)

1 clove garlic

salt and freshly ground pepper

10 oz (300 g) firm white fish fillets, such as snapper

For salad

2 teaspoons olive oil

2 tomatoes, chopped

salt and freshly ground pepper

2 tablespoons torn fresh basil leaves

1 teaspoon balsamic vinegar

Heat oven to 400°F (200°C/Gas 6).

To prepare salad, combine oil and tomatoes in bowl. Season with salt and pepper and let stand until ready to serve.

Combine all ingredients except fish in food processor and blend until just combined and mixture resembles coarse crumbs. Gently pat mixture over each fillet. Arrange fish on lightly oiled baking sheet. Bake until topping is crisp and golden, 15 to 20 minutes.

To serve, sprinkle basil and balsamic vinegar over tomatoes. Spoon onto plates with fish.

Tips

- It is important not to overprocess the coating ingredients—they will stick together if you do.

- The butter needs to be very cold to ensure a coarsely textured crumb.

- To make fresh breadcrumbs: remove crusts from white bread, cut into cubes and process in batches in food processor until crumbed. Day-old bread works best.

Peppered fish with mashed potatoes

Preparation: 10 minutes

Cooking time: 25 minutes

Serves: 4

2 tablespoons mixed peppercorns, coarsely crushed

3 tablespoons seasoned all-purpose (plain) flour

4 boneless and skinless white fish fillets, 7 oz (220 g) each

1½ lbs (750 g) waxy potatoes

2 tablespoons olive oil

6 oz (180 g) bottled artichoke hearts, drained and chopped

2 oz (60 g) chopped black olives

1 tablespoon fresh thyme leaves

¼ cup (2 fl oz/60 ml) additional olive oil

Combine crushed peppercorns and flour. Coat fillets with peppercorn mixture, pressing well into both sides. Set aside.

Peel potatoes and cut into even pieces. Boil or steam until tender. Drain and mash well. Add oil, artichoke hearts, olives and thyme and mix well. Keep warm.

Heat additional oil in large frying pan over medium-high heat and fry fish until crisp and golden, about 3 minutes on each side. Serve with warm mashed potatoes.

Poached salmon salad with soy and ginger dressing

Preparation: 5 minutes

Cooking time: 15 minutes

Serves: 2

14 oz (440 g) skinless and boneless salmon steaks

3 oz (90 g) sugar snap peas

4 asparagus stalks, cut into thirds

3½ oz (100 g) snow pea (mange tout) sprouts

¼ cup (½ oz/15 g) fresh cilantro (coriander) leaves

1 cucumber, thinly sliced

For dressing

2 tablespoons soy sauce

2 teaspoons rice vinegar or white wine vinegar

2 tablespoons Asian sesame oil

1 teaspoon finely grated fresh ginger

Steam salmon, covered, over gently simmering water 10 minutes. Remove and flake into large pieces.

Blanch snap peas and asparagus in boiling water for 1 minute. Drain and refresh under cold water. Drain well. Mix with remaining ingredients.

Whisk together dressing ingredients. Pour over vegetables and toss through.

Transfer to serving plates and pile salmon on top.

Tips

- Use a bamboo steamer or metal cake rack inside a larger saucepan to cook the salmon.

- You can microwave the asparagus and snap peas or place them in the steamer after cooking the salmon.

- If sugar snap peas aren't available, you can substitute snow peas (mange tout).

- Do not overcook the salmon. It is best when only just cooked through.

Potato and fish casserole

Preparation: 15 minutes

Cooking time: 35 minutes

Serves: 4

1½ lb (750 g) firm waxy potatoes, parboiled

1 lb (500 g) boneless, skinless cod (ling)

3 tomatoes, peeled and sliced

1 teaspoon dried basil

salt and freshly ground black pepper

3 tablespoons fish stock

5 oz (150 g) mozzarella cheese, sliced

1 oz (30 g) low-fat polyunsaturated margarine, melted

1 tomato, peeled and sliced, to serve

1 sprig fresh basil, to serve

Heat the oven to 400°F (200°C/Gas 6).

Coarsely grate the potatoes and put half into a deep ovenproof dish. Lay the fish on top, then add the tomato slices. Sprinkle with basil, season with salt and pepper and pour on the fish stock. Layer the mozzarella slices over tomato, then mix the remaining potatoes with the margarine and spread on top of the cheese.

Cook in the oven for about 35 minutes, until potato topping is crisp and browned.

Garnish with tomato slices and fresh basil.

Tip

This dish can be cooked in a microwave. Cover with microwave-safe plastic wrap pierced in a few places and microwave on medium for 15 to 18 minutes, finishing off under the broiler (grill) to brown the potatoes.

Risotto with scallops and greens

Preparation: 5 minutes

Cooking time: 30 minutes

Serves: 2

1 tablespoon butter

1 cup (7 oz/220 g) arborio or short-grain rice

1³/₄ cups (14 fl oz/450 ml) chicken stock

pinch of saffron threads (optional)

salt and freshly ground pepper

2 teaspoons olive oil

7 oz (220 g) trimmed scallops

¹/₂ cup (1 oz/30 g) fresh basil leaves

1 bunch arugula (rocket) (about 7 oz/220 g), trimmed
   and chopped

1 tablespoon lemon juice

grated lemon zest, to serve

Heat oven to 350°F (180°C/Gas 4). Heat butter in ovenproof dish with lid on stove-top or in oven. Stir in rice and set aside.

Bring chicken stock to boil in saucepan. Remove from heat and add saffron. Let stand for 2 minutes.

Pour hot stock over rice and season with salt and pepper. Bring to a boil on stovetop. Cover and bake for 20 minutes.

Meanwhile, heat oil in frying pan over high heat. Add scallops and cook for 2 to 3 minutes, stirring. Add basil, arugula and lemon juice and stir until arugula has wilted, about 1 minute.

When rice is cooked, place in bowls and top with scallop mixture. Serve garnished with lemon zest.

Tips

• This risotto uses a different method from that on pages 62 and 74 but is an equally traditional way of cooking risotto according to some. By cooking it in the oven, all the hard work is taken out—no stirring, just waiting. Do not remove the lid; that would release the steam that is cooking the rice.

• If there is a membrane still attached to the white part of the scallop, this should be removed, as should the whiter muscle that may be found on one side. The roe (orange coral) should be left intact if it is present.

Risotto with shrimp, parsley and lemon zest

Preparation: 5 minutes

Cooking time: 15 minutes

Serves: 2

3 tablespoons butter

3 scallions (spring onions/shallots), chopped

1 cup (7 oz/220 g) arborio or short-grain rice

3 cups (24 fl oz/750 ml) chicken or fish stock

pinch of saffron threads

1 tablespoon olive oil

10 oz (300 g) uncooked peeled shrimp (prawns), tails
   left intact, if desired

2 teaspoons grated lemon zest

1 tablespoon chopped fresh parsley

salt and freshly ground pepper

Melt butter in saucepan over medium heat. Add scallions and cook for 1 to 2 minutes. Add rice and stir to coat.

Meanwhile, bring stock and saffron to a boil. Add ½ cup (4 fl oz/125 ml) to rice and cook over medium heat, stirring, until stock is absorbed. Add ½ cup more stock and cook, stirring constantly, until almost all stock is absorbed. Repeat until rice is tender. For the last ½ cup, stir in stock, cover and let stand off heat.

Meanwhile, heat oil in frying pan over medium heat. Add shrimp and cook, turning, until tender, about 3 to 4 minutes. Add lemon zest, parsley and salt and pepper to taste.

Serve risotto in bowls topped with shrimp.

Tips

• An arugula (rocket) and parmesan salad makes a perfect accompaniment.

• As an alternative to risotto, serve the shrimp over hot pasta tossed in olive oil.

Roasted fish with minted green vegetables

Preparation: 15 minutes
Cooking time: 15 minutes
Serves: 4

8 oz (250 g) shelled fresh or frozen lima (broad)
beans
6 oz (180 g) shelled fresh or frozen peas
salt
1 onion, chopped
10 oz (315 g) jar artichoke hearts in oil, drained,
reserving 1½ tablespoons oil or 14 oz (440 g)
canned artichoke hearts and 1½ tablespoons olive
oil
2 tablespoons chopped fresh mint
freshly ground black pepper

4 pieces of fish (halibut, jewfish, kingfish or similar
fish) about 7 oz (220 g) each
sprigs fresh mint, to serve

Heat oven to 400°F (200°C/Gas 6).

Cook beans and peas together in lightly salted boiling
water for 5 minutes. Drain well.

Cook onion in 1 tablespoon oil (from the artichokes) until
soft. Add artichokes, beans, peas, mint and pepper. Mix
well then transfer mixture to a shallow ovenproof dish.

Lay fish on top of vegetables, completely covering them,
if possible, and brush with remaining oil. Cook in oven
for 10 minutes.

Serve garnished with mint sprigs.

Salmon with green vegetables

Preparation: 10 minutes

Serves: 2

3 oz (90 g) smoked salmon, cut into thin strips

8 asparagus spears, blanched in boiling water until tender crisp

cos lettuce, butter lettuce, or baby spinach

½ cup pine nuts, toasted

Dressing

4 tablespoons whole-egg mayonnaise or crème fraîche

2 tablespoons chives, chopped (optional)

1 teaspoon dijon mustard, to taste

Arrange salad ingredients in a bowl.

Mix together dressing ingredients and pour over salad.

Toss well and serve immediately.

Tips

- Add slices of avocado to the salad.

- Try a salad with pieces of crisp-fried bacon instead of the salmon.

- Replace the asparagus with raw strips of cucumber.

- Try it as a hot dish with pasta. Warm the salmon in a pan with 1 tablespoon white wine until the wine has almost evaporated. Add the mustard, chives, and crème fraîche and toss through pasta with the pine nuts and blanched asparagus. You could add baby spinach to the salmon in the pan if desired.

- Fresh salmon could be used if available. Sear a salmon steak in a pan with a little olive oil for about 3 minutes on each side, then break into pieces. The salmon should be only just cooked.

Sardines with black olive toast

Preparation: 10 minutes
Cooking time: 10 minutes
Serves: 4

³/₄ cup (4 oz/125 g) pitted (stoned) black olives
2 tablespoons olive oil
1 tablespoon anchovy paste (essence)
1 teaspoon Herbes de Provence or mixed herbs of
    your choice
freshly ground black pepper
16–20 fresh sardines, cleaned and scaled
4 large slices French or Italian country bread, to
    serve
lemon wedges, to serve

Put olives, oil, anchovy paste, Herbes and pepper into a blender or food processor and blend to make a thick paste.

Heat broiler (grill) on highest setting. Cook sardines under broiler for about 10 minutes, turning frequently until cooked through. Remove from the broiler and keep warm.

Toast the bread on both sides and spread the olive paste over the toast. Put the toast back under the broiler for 1 minute to heat through.

Arrange the sardines on four warmed plates and serve with the black olive toast and lemon wedges.

Scallops on the shell with basil butter sauce

Preparation: 5 minutes

Cooking time: 5 minutes

Serves: 4

24 scallops on the half shell

3 tablespoons butter

2 cloves garlic, chopped

3 tablespoons finely chopped leek

3 tablespoons finely chopped fresh basil

salt and freshly ground pepper

Preheat broiler (grill) on high. Arrange scallops on a tray.

Melt butter in frying pan over medium heat. Add garlic and leek and sauté for 1 minute, or until tender. Remove from heat and stir in basil.

Divide sauce evenly among scallops; season with salt and pepper. Place under broiler (grill) for 1 to 2 minutes, or until scallops are opaque. Serve immediately.

Tip

This recipe could also be used with oysters on the half shell.

Seafood stew with saffron and aniseed

Preparation: 15 minutes plus 1 hour standing

Cooking time: 10 minutes

Serves: 4

2 lb (1 kg) boneless seafood (see Tips)

½ cup (4 fl oz/125 ml) olive oil

⅔ cup (5 fl oz/150 ml) sweet white wine

pinch of saffron threads

3 sprigs thyme, chopped

4 oz (125 g) fennel, finely chopped

½ teaspoon finely grated orange zest

2 oz (60 g) pitted (stoned) black olives

1 tablespoon Pernod

¼ cup (2 fl oz/60 ml) mayonnaise

3 cloves garlic, pressed (crushed)

1 cup (8 oz/250 g) chopped tomato

1 tablespoon chopped flat-leaf parsley

Cut fish into 1-inch (2.5-cm) pieces (if using squid, cut it into ¾-inch (2-cm) pieces). Mix olive oil, wine, saffron, thyme, fennel, orange zest, olives and Pernod in medium bowl. Add fish and mix until well coated; if possible, let rest at room temperature for 1 hour for flavors to infuse.

Combine mayonnaise and garlic. Cover and let stand at room temperature until serving time, to allow flavors to develop.

Place fish mixture in large saucepan, cover and cook over medium heat, stirring occasionally until fish is just tender and cooked through, about 5 minutes. Let stand, covered, for 2 minutes.

Sprinkle stew with tomato and parsley and serve with a dollop of garlic mayonnaise.

Tips

• Any boneless seafood can be used, but choose varieties of a similar density so that they cook at the same speed. Try 1 lb (500 g) cod, 8 oz (250 g) scallops and 8 oz (250 g) cleaned squid.

• Pernod keeps the French theme, but another aniseed-flavored liqueur, such as Sambuca or ouzo, can be substituted.

Seared tuna steaks with Mexican salsa

Preparation: 10 minutes
Cooking time: 10 minutes
Serves: 2

1 lb (500 g) tuna steaks
1 tablespoon olive oil
juice of ½ lime
salt and freshly ground pepper

For salsa
1 large tomato, chopped
1 small purple onion, finely chopped
1 avocado, chopped
1 small chili, finely chopped, or more to taste
¼ cup cilantro (coriander) leaves, chopped
½ small red bell pepper (capsicum), chopped
2 tablespoons olive oil
juice of ½ lime
salt and freshly ground pepper
lime wedges, to serve

Brush tuna steaks with oil. Heat broiler (grill) or heavy-bottomed frying pan and sear tuna over high heat, 2 to 3 minutes on each side, depending on how rare you want it. Test by gently cutting into the middle.

Combine all salsa ingredients.

Squeeze lime juice over tuna steaks and season with salt and pepper. Serve with salsa and lime wedges.

Smoked trout pâté

Preparation: 10 minutes
Serves: 2

½ side smoked trout (5 oz/150 g), skin and bones removed
2 teaspoons lime juice
1 teaspoon grated lime zest
1 tablespoon chopped fresh dill, parsley or cilantro (coriander) leaves
¼ cup (3 oz/90 g) soft cream cheese
2 teaspoons chopped drained capers
freshly ground pepper

To serve
2 hard-cooked (boiled) eggs
baby cornichons
½ red bell pepper (capsicum), roasted then seeded, peeled and sliced
toasted rye bread
salad greens
lime wedges

Combine trout, lime juice and zest, herb and cream cheese in food processor and blend until smooth.

Add capers and ground pepper and process until just combined.

Serve pâté with eggs, cornichons, roasted red pepper, rye toast and salad greens, with lime wedges on the side.

Tips
- This recipe is suitable to use as an appetizer with crackers or toasted rye bread pieces or as a light meal with salad, eggs, cornichons and roasted pepper. The final preparation time and effort will depend on how you choose to serve it.

- Pâté can be served chilled or at room temperature, and will last 2 to 3 days if kept covered in the refrigerator.

- Smoked trout is available by the half-side in most delicatessens and some supermarkets.

Spicy clam, roasted pepper and tomato pasta

Preparation: 10 minutes

Cooking time: 30 minutes

Serves: 4

2 red bell peppers (capsicums)

6 plum (egg) tomatoes

1 lb (500 g) spaghetti

1 tablespoon olive oil

1 medium onion, finely chopped

2 cloves garlic, minced

1 small red chili, finely chopped

2 lb (1 kg) clams

¼ cup (2 fl oz/60 ml) white wine

1 tablespoon balsamic vinegar

1 tablespoon tomato paste

2 tablespoons finely chopped fresh oregano

Tips

- Almost any herb will suit this simple, light dish—try fresh cilantro (coriander), parsley, fennel, marjoram, thyme and mint.

- A word or caution: too much chili will spoil the subtle flavors of this dish.

Quarter peppers; remove seeds and membranes. Broil (grill) peppers, skin side up, until skin blisters and blackens. Transfer to plastic bag until cool enough to handle, then peel skin away. Slice peppers into thin strips. Cut tomatoes in half and place under hot broiler (grill) until lightly browned and softened, 5 to 10 minutes. Set aside.

Meanwhile, cook spaghetti in large pot of boiling salted water.

Heat oil in large saucepan over medium heat. Add onion, garlic and chili and cook, stirring, until onion is soft. Add clams and wine, cover, increase heat to high and cook, swirling pan over heat, for 5 minutes, or until clams open; discard any that do not open. Stir in peppers, vinegar, tomato paste and oregano and heat through.

Drain cooked spaghetti and serve topped with clam mixture and dotted with roasted tomatoes.

Tuna steaks with citrus salsa

Preparation: 15 minutes

Cooking time: 2 minutes

Serves: 4

1 cup (8 fl oz/250 ml) olive oil

½ bunch fresh basil

juice of 2 limes

1 medium orange

1 hothouse (continental) cucumber

1 medium-size purple onion, finely chopped

1 yellow bell pepper (capsicum), seeded and finely
   diced

4 tuna steaks, 7 oz (220 g) each

arugula (rocket) or mixed salad greens

3 tablespoons sherry vinegar

1 lime, cut into wedges, to serve

Blend or process ¾ of the oil with basil and juice of 1 lime until smooth. Set aside.

Peel and section orange; quarter the sections. Remove seeds from cucumber and finely dice flesh. Combine orange, cucumber, onion and bell pepper in a small bowl with 1 tablespoon of the remaining oil and the remaining lime juice; mix well.

Heat remaining oil in heavy frying pan and sear tuna steaks for 1 minute on each side.

Cut each steak in half and arrange on a bed of arugula or mixed greens. Top steaks with citrus salsa and drizzle with vinegar and basil oil. Serve with lime wedges.

Tips

• This simple dish is best served with steamed new potatoes.

• It is recommended that the tuna is only lightly cooked, so that it is still pink in the middle. You may prefer it cooked slightly longer.

• Grapefruit is a great alternative to orange, but if you use it, leave out the lime juice.

• For a slightly sweeter salsa, use roasted red bell pepper instead of the yellow bell pepper.

• Using a balsamic rather than sherry vinegar will also sweeten the dish slightly.

Warm scallop, fennel and eggplant salad

Preparation: 15 minutes

Cooking time: 10 minutes

Serves: 4

1 medium fennel bulb

1¼ cups (9 fl oz/270 ml) tablespoons olive oil

2 tablespoons balsamic vinegar

grated zest and juice of 1 lime

1 teaspoon brown sugar

1 lb (500 g) eggplant (aubergine)

2 teaspoons salt

2 slices bacon, chopped

1 lb (500 g) scallops, coral (orange roe) left intact if
   present, membranes removed

Remove fennel leaves from bulb and thinly slice bulb. Set leaves aside. Chop enough fennel leaves to make 1 tablespoon. Combine chopped leaves, 3 tablespoons oil, vinegar, lime zest, juice and sugar in small bowl and beat lightly until well combined.

Cut eggplant into slices ½ inch (1 cm) thick. Sprinkle with salt and place in sieve for 5 minutes to drain bitter juices. Rinse with water, then drain. Heat 3 tablespoons oil in large frying pan and cook eggplant in batches until lightly browned and tender. Keep warm.

Heat 2 tablespoons oil in same frying pan and cook fennel slices and bacon until lightly browned. Heat 1 more tablespoon oil in pan and cook scallops for 2 minutes, or until just tender.

Toss eggplant, fennel mixture and scallops together, drizzling with dressing. Serve immediately.

Tips

- To make sure salad is warm when served, make the dressing first.

- If balsamic vinegar is not available, use red wine vinegar and one more teaspoon of sugar in dressing.

chicken & turkey

THE HENLEY COLLEGE LIBRARY

Asparagus and chicken phyllo parcels

Preparation: 20 minutes
Cooking time: 40 minutes
Serves: 4

4 boneless chicken breasts
salt and pepper
2 teaspoons vegetable oil
10 sheets phyllo pastry
2 tablespoons butter, melted
2 oz (60 g) cheddar, grated
1/2 level teaspoon dried oregano
12 oz (75 g) can asparagus spears or cut asparagus
   pieces
approx. 3 tablespoons stock
1 level tablespoon cornstarch (cornflour)
3–4 tablespoons plain (natural) yogurt

Preheat oven to 400°F (200°C/Gas 6).

Trim the chicken and season lightly with salt and pepper. Heat the oil in a nonstick pan and fry the chicken until lightly browned on ach side and partly cooked through. Remove from the pan and drain well.

Brush four sheets of phyllo pastry with melted butter and place on top of one another. Halve the remaining sheets and place one in the center of each sheet of pastry. Sprinkle the cheese centrally over each pastry, then add a little oregano.

Drain the asparagus, reserving the juices, and divide half of it among the four pieces of pastry. Place a piece of chicken on each pile of asparagus. Fold pastry in to make a parcel. Turn each parcel over and place it on a baking sheet covered with nonstick baking paper. Glaze with melted butter.

Cook the parcels in the oven for 20 minutes, then reduce heat to 350°F (180°F/Gas 4) and continue cooking for 15 minutes.

Meanwhile, add enough stock to the reserved asparagus juice to make up 1¼ cups (10 fl oz/300 ml). Put in a pan and bring to a boil. Thicken with the cornstarch. Add remaining asparagus and simmer for 2 to 3 minutes. Stir in yogurt, and adjust seasoning.

Serve parcels warm with the sauce.

Avocado chicken

Preparation: 20 minutes

Cooking time: 10 minutes

Serves: 4

approx. 4 oz (125 g) fresh breadcrumbs

1 level teaspoon dried mixed herbs

4 boneless chicken breasts

salt and pepper

a little all-purpose (plain) flour for coating

1 egg, beaten

1 large or 2 small ripe avocados

grated rind of ½ lime

juice of 1 lime

4–6 tablespoons thick mayonnaise or sour cream

1 level tablespoon freshly chopped parsley

vegetable oil

slices of avocado, to serve

lemon or lime juice, to serve

lime slices, to serve

frisée or curly lettuce, to serve

Combine the breadcrumbs and mixed herbs.

Cut each chicken breast in half to give two thinner pieces. Season lightly. Dip the pieces of chicken first into flour, then into beaten egg and finally into breadcrumbs and herb mixture. Press the coating well in and chill until required.

To make sauce, thoroughly mash or puree the avocados in a food processor or blender with the lime rind and juice and then beat in the mayonnaise and parsley until evenly blended. Season to taste.

Fry the chicken portions in a shallow oil for about 4 to 5 minutes on each side, until golden brown and cooked through. Drain on paper towel. Dress with the sauce.

Serve garnished with slices of avocado dipped in lemon or lime juice, lime slice, and frisée or curly lettuce.

Tip

For a low-fat cooking method, place coated pieces of chicken on a lightly greased baking sheet and cook in a fairly hot oven 400°F(200°C/Gas 6) for 30 to 35 minutes, until cooked through, browned and crispy.

Cajun fried chicken strips with sauce remoulade

Preparation: 30 minutes

Cooking time: 10–15 minutes

Serves: 6

1 egg

¼ cup (2 fl oz/60 ml) Creole or other wholegrain
  mustard

1 teaspoon Cajun spice mix (see Tips)

¼ cup (1 oz/30 g) chopped spring (green) onions,
  including green tops

¼ cup (½ oz/15 g) chopped parsley

1 teaspoon Worcestershire sauce

¼ teaspoon or more Tabasco or other hot pepper
  sauce

1 teaspoon salt

1 cup (8 fl oz/250 ml) vegetable oil

1½ cups (6 oz/180 g) all-purpose (plain) flour

2 tablespoons Cajun spice mix, extra

2 teaspoons dried marjoram

1 teaspoon dried sage

1½ teaspoons salt

¼ teaspoon black pepper

1 egg

1 cup (8 fl oz/250 ml) milk

¼ cup (2 fl oz/60 ml) light (single) cream

6 chicken breasts, boned, skinned and cut into
  ½ x 4-inch (1 x 10-cm) strips

2–3 cups (16–24 fl oz/500–750 ml) vegetable oil

Combine egg, mustard, spice mix, spring onions, parsley, Worcestershire sauce, Tabasco and salt in a blender or food processor and pulse once or twice to mix thoroughly. With the machine running, add the oil in a slow, steady stream, blending until the sauce is smooth and creamy. Taste for salt and Tabasco and pour into a bowl. Refrigerate sauce until ready to serve.

Mix the flour, spice mix, marjoram, sage, salt and pepper in a deep plate.

Beat the egg with the milk and cream in a shallow dish or pie plate.

Soak the chicken pieces in the milk mixture for 10 to 15 minutes, turning pieces occasionally so that all are well coated. Dredge the chicken in seasoned flour and shake off excess.

Pour enough oil into a deep frying pan to come halfway up the chicken pieces and heat over high heat (a little flour sprinkled on top of oil should sizzle at the right temperature). Fry chicken over medium-high heat, turning often, for 10 to 15 minutes, or until deep golden brown. Do not burn chicken. Drain on paper towel.

Serve chicken immediately with sauce remoulade.

Tips

• To make Cajun spice mix, combine ½ cup (2 oz/60 g) paprika, ¼ cup (1 oz/30 g) black pepper, 1½ tablespoons or more, to taste, cayenne, 2 tablespoons garlic powder, 2 tablespoons onion powder and store in a closed jar in a cool, dry place. Use within a month for maximum flavor.

• Sauce remoulade can also be served with prawns, crabcakes or other seafood. It will last for up to a week in the refrigerator.

• If you prefer not to eat raw egg, you can replace it with mayonnaise. Replace egg and oil with 1 cup (8 fl oz/250 ml) good quality bottled mayonnaise.

Chicken and cashew stir-fry

Preparation: 15 minutes

Cooking time: 10 minutes

Serves: 4

2 tablespoons vegetable oil

4 oz (125 g) cashew nut kernels

1 bunch scallions (shallots/spring onions), trimmed
and sliced

4–5 sticks celery, thinly sliced

4 chicken breasts, skinned and cut into ½-inch
(1-cm) cubes

6 oz (180 g) stir-fry yellow bean sauce

salt and pepper

Using a wok or a heavy-based saucepan or skillet, heat the oil until it smokes. Toss in the cashew nuts, scallions and celery and cook for 1 to 2 minutes, stirring frequently over a fairly fierce heat until the nuts are lightly browned.

Add the chicken and cook quickly, stirring frequently for 2 to 3 minutes until sealed and just cooked. Add the yellow bean sauce, season lightly and cook for a further minute or so, until piping hot.

Serve immediately with freshly boiled rice.

Chicken and clam on bed of watercress

Preparation: 10 minutes

Cooking time: 20 minutes

Serves: 4

2 tablespoons vegetable oil

3 single chicken breast fillets (about 1½ lb/750 g)

½ cup (4 fl oz/125 ml) white wine

2 cloves garlic, minced

¼ cup (1 oz/30 g) chopped fresh oregano

1 lb (500 g) clams, rinsed

5 fl oz (150 ml) mayonnaise

grated zest and juice of 1 lime

½ bunch watercress, to serve

2 oz (60 g) sun-dried tomatoes, cut into strips, to
  serve

Heat oil in large frying pan over medium heat and cook chicken, turning occasionally, until lightly browned and cooked through. Remove from pan, cover and keep warm.

Combine wine, garlic and ½ oregano in large saucepan with lid and bring to a boil. Add clams, cover and swirl pan over high heat for about 2 minutes, or until clams open. Remove clams and let pan juices cool. Shell clams, discarding any that have not opened. Return clams to cooled pan juices.

Combine mayonnaise, lime zest and juice in small bowl and mix well.

Tear chicken into strips and place in large bowl, adding drained clams and remaining oregano. Add mayonnaise mixture and toss until chicken and clams are lightly coated.

Arrange salad on bed of watercress and sprinkle with sun-dried tomatoes.

Tip
Clams can be used instead of mussels, arugula (rocket) can be used instead of watercress, and marjoram will work just as well as oregano.

Chicken and peanut curry

Preparation: 5 minutes
Cooking time: 25 minutes
Serves: 4

1½ lbs (750 g) chicken thigh fillets
1⅔ cups (13 fl oz/400 ml) coconut cream
½ cup (4 oz/125 g) peanuts
1 clove garlic, minced
2 teaspoons ground cumin
1 teaspoon ground coriander
1 small fresh red chili, finely chopped
1 tablespoon Thai fish sauce
1 tablespoon soy sauce
1 tablespoon lime juice
2 tablespoons chopped fresh cilantro (coriander)
 leaves
cooked rice, to serve

Combine chicken and coconut cream in saucepan and bring to a boil. Simmer uncovered until chicken is tender, about 20 minutes. Drain chicken, reserving 1 cup (8 fl oz/250 ml) liquid. Slice chicken and keep warm.

While chicken is simmering, place nuts in blender or food processor and coarsely chop.

Combine garlic, cumin, ground coriander and chili in a small frying pan and stir over medium-high heat until fragrant, about 1 minute. Add reserved coconut cream, nuts, sauces and lime juice and stir until combined and heated through. Stir in 1 tablespoon coriander.

Pour sauce over chicken. Sprinkle with remaining coriander and serve with rice.

Tip

Pork loin can be used instead of chicken. You can also use sambal oelek, an Asian paste of minced chilies, instead of fresh chili if you prefer.

Chicken beanpot

Preparation: 15 minutes

Cooking time: 45 minutes

Serves: 4

8 chicken thigh joints

salt and pepper

2 tablespoons vegetable oil

1 large onion, peeled and sliced

1 clove garlic, crushed

1 level tablespoon tomato puree

15 oz (470 g) canned tomatoes

½ cup (4 fl oz/125 ml) red wine

½ level teaspoon ground allspice

15 oz (470 g) canned red kidney beans, drained

chopped parsley, to serve

Preheat oven to 350°F (180°C/Gas 4).

Trim the chicken and season lightly. Heat the oil in a pan and fry the chicken until browned. Transfer to a shallow casserole.

Fry the onion and garlic in the same oil until golden brown, then pour off any excess oil from the pan. Add the tomato puree, tomatoes, wine, and allspice and bring to a boil. Add the beans and pour mixture over the chicken.

Cover the casserole and cook in the oven for about 45 minutes, or until tender.

When cooked, adjust seasonings, sprinkle with chopped parsley, and serve with boiled rice or pasta and a salad.

Tip

To cook in a microwave, place in a microwave dish and cook on maximum (100%) for 6 minutes; turn over chicken thighs and cook for a further 6 to 7 minutes.

Chicken breast baked on mushrooms with parsnip puree

Preparation: 5 minutes

Cooking time: 40 minutes

Serves: 2

2 teaspoons butter

2 teaspoons olive oil

10 oz (300 g) mushrooms, sliced

2 tablespoons chopped scallions (shallots/spring onions)

¼ cup (2 fl oz/60 ml) white wine

¼ cup (2 fl oz/60 ml) heavy (double) cream

salt and freshly ground pepper

1 whole chicken breast (about 14 oz/440 g)

1 teaspoon fresh thyme leaves or ½ teaspoon dried

2 parsnips (about 7 oz/220 g), peeled and chopped into 1¼ inch (3 cm) pieces

2 teaspoons butter

¼ cup (2 fl oz/60 ml) milk or cream

salt and freshly ground pepper

Heat oven to 350°F (180°C/Gas 4).

Heat butter and oil in ovenproof pan with lid and cook mushrooms and scallions over medium heat on stovetop, partially covered, for 5 minutes. Stir in wine and cream and bring to a boil. Season with salt and pepper.

Place chicken over mushrooms and sprinkle with thyme. Cover and bake until chicken is cooked through, 20 to 30 minutes.

Meanwhile, boil parsnips until tender. Place in blender or food processor with remaining ingredients and puree until smooth.

Serve parsnip puree with chicken and mushrooms.

Tip

This dish is especially appealing when made with several mixed varieties of mushrooms.

Chicken pilaf

Preparation: 5 minutes
Cooking time: 30 minutes
Serves: 4

2 chicken thigh fillets
1 whole chicken breast
3 teaspoons turmeric
2 tablespoons olive oil
seeds from 8 cardamom pods
1 small carrot, finely diced
1 small parsnip, finely diced
3 cloves garlic, pressed (crushed)
1 cup (7 oz/220 g) long-grain rice
2 large tomatoes, peeled and diced
2 cups (16 fl oz/500 ml) chicken stock
2 tablespoons chopped fresh mint, to serve

Toss chicken with 2 teaspoons turmeric in plastic bag.
Heat 1 tablespoon oil in large frying pan over medium-high
heat. Add chicken and cook, turning occasionally until
browned all over. Remove from pan.

Heat remaining oil in same pan over medium heat. Add
cardamom, carrot, parsnip and garlic and cook for
5 minutes, being careful not to overcook garlic. Add rice
and continue cooking 5 minutes, stirring frequently.

Cut chicken into bite-size chunks and add to rice mixture.
Add tomatoes, stock and remaining turmeric, cover and
simmer gently until rice is cooked through, about
20 minutes. Sprinkle with mint and serve.

Tips

• A medium- or short-grain rice gives a softer texture;
  brown rice will take about 15 minutes longer to cook.

• A mixture of thigh and breast meat gives the most
  robust flavor, but you can use four of either.

• If parsnip is not available, use another carrot or some
  turnip or squash.

Chicken texacano

Preparation: 10 minutes

Cooking time: 55 minutes

Serves: 4

4 partly-boned chicken breasts

1 clove garlic, crushed

2 level tablespoons tomato puree

1 tablespoon clear honey

1/2 level teaspoon dry mustard

2–3 good dashes Tabasco (hot pepper) sauce

salt

3 oz (90 g) raisins

2/3 cup (6 fl oz/180 ml) stock

1 oz (30 g) sunflower seeds

Preheat oven to 400°F (200°C/Gas 6).

Rub the pieces of chicken liberally with garlic and place in a shallow ovenproof dish.

Combine the tomato puree, honey, mustard, Tabasco sauce and a pinch of salt and spread over the pieces of chicken. Sprinkle chicken with the raisins.

Bring the stock to the boil and pour over the chicken. Cover the dish and cook in the oven for 40 minutes.

Remove the lid, baste once with the juice, sprinkle with the sunflower seeds and return to the oven, uncovered, for about 15 minutes, until cooked through.

Serve with freshly boiled rice and a salad.

Tips

• This dish can be prepared as far as sprinkling with raisins then chilled until ready to cook.

• Eight chicken thigh joints may be used in place of the breast, in which case cut the initial cooking time by 10 minutes.

Chicken with kumquats

Preparation: 15 minutes

Cooking time: 35 minutes

Serves: 4

4 chicken breasts or supremes of chicken

salt and pepper

3 tablespoons (1½ oz/45 g) butter or margarine

¾ cup (6 fl oz/180 ml) white wine

⅓ cup (3 fl oz/90 ml) stock

1 tablespoon lemon juice

3 oz (90 g) kumquats

2 oz (60 g) walnut halves, halved

1½ tablespoons clear honey

1 tablespoon cornstarch (cornflour)

2 tablespoons brandy

watercress, to serve

Remove any skin from the chicken pieces and season lightly. Heat the butter in a pan and fry the pieces of chicken gently for about 3 minutes on each side, until golden brown and almost cooked through. Add the wine, stock, lemon juice and seasonings and bring to a boil.

Reserve four kumquats for garnish. Slice remaining kumquats and add to the pan with the walnuts and honey. Simmer, covered, for 8 to 10 minutes, until tender. Thicken the sauce with the cornstarch blended in a little cold water, bring back to a boil and simmer for a minute or so.

Pour the brandy over the chicken and ignite. Adjust the seasoning.

Serve each portion of chicken with sauce spooned over. Garnish with a whole kumquat and sprig of watercress.

Chicken with white bean puree and antipasti

Preparation: 5 minutes

Cooking time: 20 minutes

Serves: 2

2 tablespoons (1 oz/30 g) butter

2 cloves garlic, minced

7 oz (220 g) can white beans such as cannellini,
   drained and rinsed

2 tablespoons light (single) cream

salt and freshly ground pepper

1 tablespoon lemon juice

1 tablespoon olive oil

13 oz (400 g) chicken tenderloins

4 slices prosciutto

4 marinated artichoke hearts, to serve

black olives, to serve

roasted red bell pepper (capsicum), to serve

Melt butter in frying pan. Add garlic and beans and cook over medium heat, 2 to 3 minutes. Puree bean mixture in blender or food processor with cream and salt and pepper to taste.

Combine lemon juice and olive oil. Chargrill or broil (grill) chicken tenderloins at medium heat for 3 to 4 minutes on each side, brushing with olive oil mixture.

Broil (grill) prosciutto until crisp.

Serve chicken and prosciutto with bean puree, artichokes, olives and roasted peppers.

Tips

- Serve the juicy chicken pieces and crispy prosciutto with a selection of delicious antipasti bought from the delicatessen. Artichokes, olives and bell peppers are suggested here, but you could try marinated eggplant (aubergine) and mushrooms.

- The bell peppers you buy at the delicatessen will probably be marinated in olive oil but you can roast a red bell pepper yourself and cut it into strips.

Coq au vin

Preparation: 10 minutes
Cooking time: 30 minutes
Serves: 2

1 tablespoon olive oil
14 oz (440 g) boneless, skinless chicken thigh fillets,
    cut into 1½-inch (3-cm) pieces
½ small leek, sliced
1 small carrot, sliced
1 celery stalk, sliced
3½ oz (100 g) mushrooms
1 cup (8 fl oz/250 ml) dry white wine
1 cup (8 fl oz/250 ml) chicken stock
salt and freshly ground pepper
1 tablespoon chopped fresh parsley
cooked noodles or rice, to serve

Heat 2 teaspoons oil in saucepan and brown chicken pieces on all sides over medium heat, about 2 to 3 minutes. Remove and set aside.

Heat remaining oil. Add leek, carrot, celery and mushrooms and cook over low heat, partially covered, for 5 minutes, stirring occasionally.

Return chicken to pan with wine and stock. Bring to boil, reduce heat and simmer for 15 to 20 minutes.

Season to taste with salt and pepper and stir in parsley. Serve with hot noodles or rice.

Coujons of chicken with tartare sauce

Preparation: 20 minutes

Cooking time: 20 minutes

Serves: 4

4 boneless breasts of chicken

small amount of all-purpose (plain) flour

1–2 eggs, beaten

golden or dried breadcrumbs

vegetable oil

1 cup (8 fl oz/250 ml) low-fat mayonnaise

2–3 tablespoons low-fat natural yogurt

1 level tablespoon capers, chopped

2–3 gherkins, finely chopped

8 stuffed green olives, finely chopped

1 clove garlic, pressed (crushed) (optional)

2 level tablespoons chopped chives or 2 level
tablespoons chopped scallions (shallots/spring
  onions) or raw onion

1–2 level tablespoons freshly chopped parsley

finely grated rind of ¼ lemon or ½ lime

lemon or lime quarters or wedges, to serve

watercress or parsley, to serve

Remove the skin from the chicken and cut chicken into approx. 2 x ¾-inch (5 x 2-cm) strips. Coat lightly in flour then dip into beaten egg and finally coat in breadcrumbs. Chill until ready to serve.

Combine mayonnaise, yogurt, capers, gherkins, olives, garlic, chives, parsley and lemon rind, adding seasonings to taste. Place in a bowl, cover and let stand for the flavors to marry for at least an hour before serving.

Bake chicken in the oven for 20 to 30 minutes, until golden brown and crisp.

Serve hot or cold, garnished with lemon or lime quarters or wedges and watercress or parsley.

Crispy chicken

Preparation: 5 minutes plus 20 minutes refrigeration

Cooking time: 10–15 minutes

Serves: 4

4 skinned, boned chicken breast halves or thighs

¼ cup (1 oz/30 g) all-purpose (plain) flour

salt and freshly ground black pepper

1 egg

1 tablespoon milk

1 cup (4 oz/125 g) dried breadcrumbs

2 tablespoon vegetable oil

Rinse and dry chicken with paper towel.

Place flour in a plastic bag. Season with salt and pepper; shake to mix. Spread onto a shallow dish. Place egg and milk in another shallow dish and, using a fork, beat to combine. Place breadcrumbs on a third dish.

Using tongs, coat chicken on both sides in flour, dip into egg then press into breadcrumbs to coat evenly. Place on a plate lined with greaseproof (waxed) paper, and refrigerate for 20 minutes to set coating.

Heat butter and oil in a large, heavy-based frying pan over medium heat until butter stops foaming. Add chicken and cook for 5 to 8 minutes on each side, or until tender and golden. Serve immediately.

Tips

- To oven-fry: preheat oven to 350°F (180°C/Gas 4). Place chicken in a lightly greased baking dish, cover and bake for 15 minutes. Turn chicken over, re-cover and bake for 10 minutes. Remove cover and bake for 10 to 15 minutes, or until cooked and golden.

- Powdered herbs and spices can be added to the flour. Try a pinch of cayenne pepper, paprika, ground cumin, curry powder, dried sage, oregano or dill, or finely grated lemon rind.

- To make homemade dried breadcrumbs: place 4 slices white sandwich bread on a baking sheet and bake at 300°F (150°C/Gas 2), turning occasionally, for 12 to 15 minutes, or until dry and golden. Let cool then process in a blender or food processor until finely crumbed. Store in an airtight container.

Curried chicken casserole

Preparation: 10 minutes

Cooking time: 35–45 minutes

Serves: 4–6

3 lb (1.5 kg) chicken, cut into pieces

¼ cup (1 oz/30 g) all-purpose (plain) flour

¾ teaspoon salt

¼ teaspoon freshly ground black pepper

¼ teaspoon paprika

1 clove garlic

1 small onion

1 small green bell pepper (capsicum)

2 oz (60 g) butter

2 teaspoons curry powder or curry paste

½ teaspoon dried thyme

14 oz (440 g) can whole, peeled tomatoes, undrained
 and crushed

3 tablespoons dried currants or chopped seedless
raisins

3 tablespoons chopped fresh parsley or cilantro
 (coriander) leaves

¼ cup sliced almonds

cooked rice or couscous, to serve

fruit chutney, to serve

Rinse chicken pieces under cold running water and dry
with paper towel.

Place flour, salt, pepper and paprika in a plastic bag or container. Place 1 or 2 chicken pieces at a time into bag, seal and shake to coat.

Peel and finely chop garlic and onion. Halve bell pepper, remove seeds and cut into ¼-inch (5-mm) squares.

Melt butter in a large, heavy-based frying pan over medium heat until foaming subsides. Add chicken, in batches, and cook for 1 to 2 minutes each side or until brown. Transfer cooked chicken to a plate. Drain excess fat from pan, leaving 1 to 2 tablespoons fat with cooking juices.

Add garlic, onion and bell pepper to pan and cook, stirring, over medium heat for 3 to 5 minutes, or until onion is golden. Add remaining ingredients except chicken and almonds and bring to a boil.

Return chicken to pan and cover. Reduce heat and simmer gently for 20 to 30 minutes or until chicken is tender.

Just before serving, roast almonds in a dry, nonstick frying pan over medium heat, stirring occasionally until brown.

Serve chicken on rice or couscous, sprinkled with almonds and accompanied by fruit chutney.

Gingered chicken

Preparation: 10 minutes

Cooking time: 25 minutes

Serves: 4

4 boneless chicken breasts

salt and pepper

3 tablespoons (1½ oz/45 g) butter or margarine

4 pieces stem ginger in syrup, chopped

grated rind of 1 lemon

juice of 1 lemon

3–4 tablespoons sherry

shredded crisp lettuce

chopped scallions (shallots/spring onions), to serve

fried bread croutons, to serve

Remove any skin from chicken and cut the flesh into strips. Season lightly.

Melt the butter in a pan and fry the chicken briskly until lightly browned and cooked almost though, about 10 minutes. Add the ginger, ginger syrup, lemon rind and juice, and sherry and bring slowly to a boil. Simmer gently for 3 to 4 minutes then adjust the seasonings.

Serve on a bed of shredded lettuce sprinkled with scallions and garnished with fried bread croutons.

Tip

To make fried bread croutons, cut slices of brown or white bread into crescents or half moons using a 2½-inch (6-cm) fluted cutter: first cut a circle and then take a 'bite' out of it to give the crescent. Fry in shallow oil for 2 to 3 minutes on each side until browned, then drain on paper towel.

Lyonnaise chicken

Preparation: 15 minutes
Cooking time: 25 minutes
Serves: 4

4 boneless breasts of chicken, skinned
salt and pepper
²/₃ cup (5 fl oz/150 ml) chicken stock
2 tablespoons vegetable oil
3 onions, peeled and thinly sliced
1–2 cloves garlic, pressed (crushed)
2 lb (1 kg) potatoes, peeled and parboiled
2 level teaspoons freshly chopped thyme or 1 level
   teaspoon dried thyme
watercress, to serve

Cut the pieces of chicken into narrow strips and season lightly. Poach chicken in a nonstick pan in the stock for about 5 minutes, stirring frequently until cooked through. Drain and keep warm.

Heat the fat in a pan, add the onions and garlic and fry very gently until soft but not coloured.

Cut the potatoes into about ³/₄-inch (2-cm) dice, add to the onions and fry until browned all over, stirring from time to time.

Return the chicken pieces to the pan with the thyme and plenty of seasonings. Allow to heat through thoroughly and stir to mix well. Serve at once garnished with watercress.

Tip

Sliced gerkins (4 to 6) or 8 to 12 black or stuffed green olives can be added to onions.

Moroccan-style chicken, lemon and olive pie

Preparation: 10 minutes plus 10 minutes thawing
Cooking time: 35 minutes
Serves: 2

2 teaspoons olive oil
1 clove garlic, minced
1 small onion, sliced
14 oz (440 g) boneless chicken thighs, cut into
  pieces
½ preserved lemon (pith removed), rinsed and
  chopped
½ teaspoon ground cumin
1 large tomato, chopped
1 zucchini (courgette), sliced
½ cup (4 fl oz/125 ml) chicken stock
¼ cup (½ oz/15 g) chopped flat-leaf parsley or
  cilantro (coriander) leaves
about 8 Kalamata or other medium-size black olives
2 sheets prepared pie pastry
1 egg, beaten

Preheat oven to 350°F (180°C/Gas 4). Heat oil in saucepan over medium heat. Add garlic and onion and cook for 5 minutes.

Add chicken, lemon, cumin, tomato and zucchini and for cook 5 more minutes, stirring occasionally. Add stock and bring to a boil. Stir in parsley and olives.

Divide mixture between two 12 oz (375 g) ovenproof dishes, 4 to 6 inches (10 to 15 cm) in diameter. Top each with pastry round, trimming it to overlap edges slightly. Pinch pastry edge and cut hole in top. Brush with a little beaten egg.

Bake until pastry is golden, about 25 minutes.

Tips

• Preserved lemons are available in jars at Middle Eastern markets. It is the skin that is used to add a unique tangy flavor to dishes. Remove and discard the pith and rinse the skin well.

• Use shortcrust or puff pastry which can be bought frozen and thawed before use.

Peanut and chicken croquettes

Preparation: 20 minutes

Cooking time: 15 minutes

Serves: 4–6

½ cup (4 oz/125 g) butter or margarine

1 cup (4 oz/125 g) all-purpose (plain) flour

2½ cups (20 fl oz/625 ml) milk

salt and pepper

½ level teaspoon ground coriander

¾–1 lb (375–500 g) cooked chicken meat, minced

2 oz (60 g) peanuts, chopped

2 level tablespoons chopped parsley

1 level tablespoon freshly chopped mixed herbs or
   1 level teaspoon dried mixed herbs

grated rind of 1 orange

a little seasoned all-purpose (plain) flour

1 egg, beaten

dried breadcrumbs

vegetable oil

tomato wedges, to serve

watercress or parsley sprigs, to serve

Melt the butter in a pan, stir in the flour and cook for a few minutes. Gradually add the milk and bring slowly to the boil. Simmer for 2 to 3 minutes until really thick, then remove from the heat and beat in plenty of seasoning and the coriander. Leave to cool.

Add the chicken meat, peanuts, herbs, and orange rind and then chill for about 30 minutes.

Divide mixture into eight or twelve pieces and form into croquettes or flat cakes. Dip into seasoned flour, then into beaten egg, and finally coat in the breadcrumbs.

Fry in deep hot oil (350°F/180°C), several at a time, for about 5 minutes, or until golden brown. Drain well and serve hot, garnished with tomato wedges and sprigs of watercress or parsley.

Pickled chicken pies

Preparation: 15 to 20 minutes
Cooking time: 35 to 40 minutes
Serves: 4

2 cups (8 oz/250 g) all-purpose (plain) flour
pinch of salt
¼ cup (2 oz/60 g) butter or block margarine
¼ cup (2 oz/60 g) lard or white fat
cold water to mix
1 lb (500 g) chicken breast or thigh, diced
1 small onion, peeled and finely chopped
1 carrot, peeled and coarsely grated
salt and pepper
2 level tablespoons chunky pickle or chutney
2 level tablespoons thick mayonnaise or sour cream
beaten egg or milk, to glaze
sesame seeds

Preheat oven to 400°F (200°C/Gas 6).

Sift the flour and salt into a bowl and rub in the butter and lard until mixture resembles fine breadcrumbs. Add sufficient water to mix to a pliable dough and knead lightly until smooth.

Combine the chicken, onion, carrot, seasonings, pickle or chutney and mayonnaise. Roll out two-thirds of the pastry and use to line five individual pie or Yorkshire pudding pans about 4½ inches (11 cm) in diameter.

Divide the filling among these pans then roll out the remaining pastry and cut into lids to fit the pans. Damp the edges of pastry in pans, position lids and press well together. Crimp the edges, glaze with beaten egg or milk and sprinkle with sesame seeds. Make three holes in each lid.

Cook in the oven for 25 minutes, then reduce heat to 350°F (180°C/Gas 4) and continue to cook for 10 to 15 minutes until golden brown. Serve hot or cold.

Poached chicken breast in creamy garlic sauce

Preparation: 5 minutes

Cooking time: 15 minutes

Serves: 4

4 chicken breast fillets, about 7 to 8 oz (220 to
    250 g) each

²/₃ cup (5 fl oz/150 ml) white wine

6 tablespoons water

4 oz (125 g) soft cream cheese

2 cloves garlic, minced

1 tablespoon chopped fresh tarragon

1 tablespoon chopped fresh sage

Trim chicken fillets of all excess fat. Combine chicken, wine and water in saucepan. Cover and cook over medium heat until chicken is cooked through, about 8 minutes.

Stir in cheese and garlic and cook, stirring, until cheese melts and sauce is thickened, about 5 minutes. Stir in herbs until well combined. Serve immediately.

Seared chicken livers with toast and bacon

Preparation: 5 minutes

Cooking time: 10 minutes

Serves: 2

2 slices bacon, cut in half

1 tablespoon butter

2 teaspoons olive oil

3 scallions (spring onions/shallots), chopped

14 oz (440 g) chicken livers, trimmed

salt and freshly ground pepper

3 fresh sage leaves, sliced

2 tablespoons white or red wine vinegar

¼ cup (2 fl oz/60 ml) crème fraîche

4 thick slices bread, toasted and buttered, to serve

Broil (grill) bacon.

Meanwhile, heat butter and oil in frying pan. Add scallions and cook over medium heat for 3 minutes. Remove with slotted spoon and set aside.

Reheat pan and cook livers over medium-high heat 5 minutes, turning occasionally. Sprinkle with salt, pepper and sage. Remove and set aside.

Add vinegar and deglaze pan by cooking over high heat, stirring up any remaining brown bits. Stir in crème fraîche and boil for 1 minute. Return scallions and livers to pan and reheat for 1 minute.

Serve livers on buttered toast with bacon.

Tips

• This light meal would be finished off perfectly with a simple green salad.

• If crème fraîche cannot be found, sour cream can be used instead.

Simple chicken sauté

Preparation: 2 minutes

Cooking time: 25–30 minutes

Serves: 4

4 boneless, skinned chicken breast fillets or 2½ lb
(1.25 kg) chicken, cut into 8 pieces

freshly ground black pepper

2 tablespoons butter

1 tablespoon vegetable or olive oil

½ cup (4 fl oz/125 ml) chicken stock, dry white wine
or water

2 tablespoons Dijon mustard

1 teaspoon wholegrain (seeded) mustard (optional)

¾ cup (6 fl oz/180 ml) whipping cream

Rinse chicken under cold running water and dry with
paper towel. Sprinkle with pepper to taste.

Heat butter and oil in a large, heavy-based frying pan
over medium heat. When foaming subsides, add
chicken and cook for 5 to 6 minutes on each side or until
golden brown.

Cover pan, reduce heat and cook for 8 to 10 minutes, or
until chicken is just tender—pieces on the bone take
longer than fillets. Using tongs, transfer chicken to a
heated serving platter and cover loosely with foil
to keep warm.

For sauce, drain excess fat from pan, leaving 1 to
2 tablespoons fat with cooking juices. Add stock,
mustards and cream to pan, and mix well over medium
heat. Bring to a boil and simmer, stirring occasionally,
5 minutes or until sauce reduces and thickens slightly.
Pour sauce over chicken and serve immediately.

Tips

• To cut up (section) a chicken: using a sharp knife, cut
  skin where leg joins body, then cut through joint
  between thigh and body to remove leg. Cut through
  drumstick and thigh joint. Bend wing away from body,
  cut through joint, taking a small amount of breast meat
  with wing. Cut off wing tips. Cut through ribs on both
  sides of body to separate breast from back. Position
  breast, skin side down, and using a heavy knife or
  cleaver, cut breastbone in half lengthwise. If still large,
  cut pieces in half crosswise too. Trim off excess fat,
  skin and small bones from all pieces. Discard. Freeze
  back section and wing tips for stock.

• For a mushroom sauce: slice 4 oz (125 g) button
  mushrooms and cook with chicken. Use chicken stock
  instead of wine or water and substitute 2 tablespoons
  dry sherry for mustard.

Spiced chicken

Preparation: 30 minutes

Cooking time: 10 minutes

Serves: 4

2 teaspoons ginger, minced

2 cloves garlic, minced

1 teaspoon salt

$\frac{1}{2}$ teaspoon ground black pepper

1 teaspoon cumin

1 teaspoon paprika

2 teaspoons ground coriander

2 tablespoons flat-leaf parsley or cilantro (coriander) leaves, chopped (optional)

2 tablespoons lemon juice

3 tablespoons oil

2 whole chicken breasts or 4 halves, skin removed

Combine spices, juice, and oil to make a paste. Rub into chicken and let stand for as long as possible.

Heat broiler (grill) or cast-iron grill pan and cook chicken for about 5 minutes each side, until cooked through.

Serve hot or chilled.

Tips

- You can cut the meat into bite-size chunks and thread onto skewers before cooking.

- The chicken can also be roasted, although this is best with pieces on the bone or even with a whole chicken. It is a longer process but equally hassle-free. Place in a baking dish and cook in a preheated 350°F (180°C/ Gas 4) oven for about 45 minutes.

- Use yogurt instead of oil for a creamy, low-fat marinade.

- Experiment with different ground spice blends: try adding 1 teaspoon each curry powder, garam masala, and/or minced chili. For a Caribbean variation, use $\frac{1}{2}$ teaspoon allspice, $\frac{1}{4}$ teaspoon thyme, $\frac{1}{2}$ teaspoon salt, big pinch cinnamon, 2 crushed garlic cloves, 1 tablespoon soy sauce, 1 tablespoon water, $\frac{1}{4}$ teaspoon minced ginger and minced chili to taste.

Stilton sauce-topped chicken

Preparation: 15 minutes

Cooking time: 35 minutes

Serves: 4

4 boneless chicken breasts or supremes of chicken

about 2 tablespoons seasoned all-purpose (plain)
  flour

2 tablespoon (1 oz/30 g) butter or margarine

1 tablespoon vegetable oil

1 small onion, peeled and finely chopped

1¼ cups (10 fl oz/ 300 ml) stock

3 tablespoons sherry

1 tablespoon lemon juice

3 oz (90 g) Stilton cheese, crumbled or grated

1 level tablespoon finely chopped gherkins

3 oz (90 g) seedless white grapes

salt and pepper

gherkin fans, to serve

white grapes, to serve

Remove the skin from the chicken and coat chicken lightly in seasoned flour. Heat the butter and oil in a pan and fry the pieces of chicken for about 7 to 8 minutes on each side, until almost cooked through. Drain and keep warm.

Spoon off all but 1 tablespoon oil from the pan, add the onion and fry gently until soft. Stir in 1 tablespoon of the remaining seasoned flour and cook for a minute or so.

Gradually add the stock and bring to a boil. Add the sherry, lemon juice and cheese and heat until cheese is melted.

Return the chicken to the pan with the gherkins and grapes and season to taste. Simmer for 4 to 5 minutes.

Arrange the chicken on a serving dish, spoon the sauce over and garnish with gherkin fans and small bunches of grapes.

Stir-fried chicken and vegetables with noodles

Preparation: 5 minutes

Cooking time: 10 minutes

Serves: 4

1 lb (500 g) package fresh Chinese or Japanese thick
wheat (Hokkien) noodles

1 tablespoon vegetable oil

1 tablespoon Asian sesame oil

1 tablespoon finely grated fresh ginger

3 cloves garlic, minced

1 small red chili, finely chopped

1 lb (500 g) lean ground chicken

1 medium onion, thinly sliced

1 lb (500 g) mixed Chinese vegetables (bok choy,
Chinese broccoli, bean sprouts, baby corn, snow
peas)

¼ cup (2 fl oz/60 ml) soy sauce

1 tablespoon black bean sauce

1 tablespoon oyster sauce

Cook noodles according to package instructions. Drain
and set aside.

Heat oils in wok or large frying pan. Add ginger, garlic, chili
and chicken and stir-fry for 2 minutes or until chicken is
lightly browned.

Add onion and mixed vegetables and stir-fry for 1 minute.

Stir in sauces and noodles and stir-fry 2 for 2 minutes, to
mix and heat through.

Tips

• Thinner egg noodles can be used instead of the thick
wheat noodles if you prefer.

• If further heat is required, add a tablespoon of sweet
chili sauce.

• For a slightly smokier flavor, swap the black bean sauce
for hoisin sauce.

Stroganoff-style chicken

Preparation: 15 minutes

Cooking time: 35 to 40 minutes

Serves: 4

4 boneless chicken breasts

2 tablespoons light oil

2 onions, peeled and thinly sliced

1 red bell pepper (capsicum), seeded and sliced

1 green bell pepper (capsicum) seeded and sliced

4 oz (125 g) button mushroom, trimmed and sliced

1 level tablespoon dried thyme

4 tablespoons stock or white wine

salt and pepper

$^2/_3$ cup (5 fl oz/150 ml) sour cream or low-fat plain
  (natural) yogurt

freshly chopped parsley, to garnish

Cut the chicken into strips. Heat half the oil in a nonstick pan and fry the pieces briskly until lightly browned and cooked through. Remove from the pan.

Put the rest of the oil in the pan, add the onions and fry gently until soft, about 7 to 8 minutes. Add the bell peppers and cook gently for 3 to 4 minutes; then add the mushrooms and continue for a further 2 to 3 minutes.

Return the chicken to the pan with the herbs, stock and seasonings, bring to a boil and simmer for 2 to 3 minutes. Stir in the sour cream and reheat gently.

Adjust seasonings and serve sprinkled with plenty of chopped parsley on a bed of boiled rice or pasta.

Stuffed chicken breasts wrapped in prosciutto

Preparation: 10 minutes

Cooking time: 30 minutes

Serves: 4

4 medium chicken breast fillets

4 oz (125 g) camembert, sliced

2 teaspoons fresh thyme leaves or 1 teaspoon dried

8 thin slices prosciutto

2 tablespoons olive oil

8 scallions (spring onions/shallots), finely chopped

¼ cup (2 fl oz/60 ml) white wine

½ cup (4 fl oz/125 ml) heavy (double) cream

Cut shallow slit into sides of chicken breasts and stuff each fillet with 2 or 3 slices of cheese. Sprinkle fillets with thyme, wrap with prosciutto and secure with toothpicks.

Heat oil in large frying pan over medium heat. Add chicken fillets and cook until tender and lightly browned, about 10 minutes on each side. Remove chicken from pan and keep warm.

Return pan to heat. Add scallions to juices and cook, stirring, until soft. Add wine and cream and simmer until heated through and slightly thickened, about 5 minutes. Serve chicken drizzled with sauce.

Turkey, beet and potato salad with herb dressing

Preparation: 10 minutes

Cooking time: 20 minutes

Serves: 4

1½ lbs (750 g) potatoes, peeled

8 oz (250 g) smoked turkey breast

2 cans (1 lb/500 g each) whole baby beets (beetroot), drained, halved

2 purple onions, sliced

2 oz (60 g) watercress sprigs

½ cup (4 fl oz/125 ml) sour cream

1 tablespoon balsamic vinegar

1 tablespoon cream

1 tablespoon chopped fresh thyme

Cut potatoes into 1-inch (2.5-cm) cubes and boil until just tender. Drain, rinse under cold water and drain again.

Slice turkey into thin strips. Combine potatoes, turkey, beets, onion and watercress in salad bowl and toss gently.

Combine sour cream, vinegar, cream and thyme in small bowl and mix well. Serve salad drizzled with dressing.

Tips

- You can use chicken if you prefer for this hearty meal.

- If you find the dressing too thick, stir in 1 tablespoon of water.

Turkey, cherry tomato and bacon frittata

Preparation: 5 minutes
Cooking time: 20 minutes
Serves: 4

8 slices bacon
12 cherry tomatoes, halved
12 eggs
¼ cup (2 fl oz/60 ml) thickened cream or heavy
   (double) cream
¼ cup (2 oz/60 g) butter
6 oz (180 g) sliced turkey breast, chopped
¼ cup (1 oz/30 g) chopped fresh chives

Preheat oven to 400°F (200°C/Gas 4).

Place bacon in roasting pan and bake for 10 minutes or until just beginning to crisp. Set aside.

Reduce oven temperature to 325°F (170°C/Gas 3).

Beat eggs with cream in medium bowl until well combined. Lightly oil large ovenproof frying pan. Melt butter in oiled pan over medium heat. Add egg mixture and cook, stirring gently, for 1 minute. Reduce heat and cook for 3 minutes without stirring, or until bottom is set and lightly browned.

Place pan in oven until egg is just set, about 4 minutes.

To serve, arrange tomatoes around edge of pan. Chop bacon into ¾-inch (2-cm) pieces, combine with turkey and sprinkle over center of hot frittata. Scatter with chopped chives. Serve in wedges.

beef, lamb & pork

Beef and pecan stir-fry

Preparation: 10 minutes

Cooking time: 10 minutes

Serves: 4

12 oz (375 g) thin fresh egg noodles

1 lb (500 g) beef tenderloin

1 tablespoon vegetable oil

2 teaspoons Asian sesame oil

1 tablespoon minced fresh ginger

3 cloves garlic, pressed (crushed)

2 small red chilies, finely chopped

3 tablespoons oyster sauce

2 tablespoons soy sauce

13 oz (400 g) bok choy, coarsely chopped

12 scallions (shallots/spring onions), sliced

1 medium carrot, cut into thin julienne

1/4 cup (1 oz/30 g) chopped fresh cilantro (coriander) leaves

3/4 cup (3 oz/90 g) chopped pecans

Boil noodles until just tender. Cut beef into thin strips.

Heat oils in wok or large frying pan until just smoking. Add meat in batches and cook until browned and tender, about 2 minutes per batch. Return all meat to pan.

Stir in ginger, garlic, chilies and sauces and stir-fry for 2 minutes, or until fragrant.

Stir in remaining ingredients, including noodles, and cook, stirring, until heated through, about 2 to 3 minutes. Serve immediately.

Tips

• There are two secrets to a good stir-fry: have the pan or wok very hot, and don't cook anything too long. This will keep the meat tender and the vegetables crisp.

• Any style of noodles can be used, dried or fresh, and the vegetables can be changed as desired. But remember to cut all vegetables into thin or small pieces so they need only brief cooking.

Beef koftas and salad in pita pockets

Preparation: 10 minutes

Cooking time: 5–8 minutes

Serves: 4

1 medium onion, grated

2 cloves garlic, minced

2 oz (60 g) pine nuts, toasted and finely chopped

1 lb (500 g) lean ground (minced) beef

2 tablespoons chopped fresh mint

1 teaspoon ground cumin

1 egg, lightly beaten

2 tablespoons olive oil

3 tablespoons lemon juice

1/2 teaspoon finely grated lemon zest

mixed salad greens e.g. arugula (rocket), romaine (cos) and watercress

4 large wholewheat (wholemeal) pita breads, if desired

Combine onion, garlic, pine nuts, meat, mint, cumin and egg in large bowl and mix well. Shape mixture into small sausage shapes and push onto skewers. Broil (grill) under medium heat, turning regularly, for 5 to 8 minutes, or until browned and cooked through.

Combine oil, lemon juice and zest in medium bowl and toss with greens. Serve pitas stuffed with generous quantities of greens and several koftas.

Tips

- If you prefer, the koftas can be panfried in olive oil; broiling (grilling) is a leaner alternative.

- If using wooden skewers, soak them in water for 15 minutes to prevent them burning.

- You can use lamb or chicken instead of beef.

- Although mint gives a more Middle Eastern flavor, flat-leaf parsley tastes just as good.

Beef stroganoff

Preparation: 5 minutes
Cooking time: 15 minutes
Serves: 2

1 tablespoon olive oil
½ small onion, sliced
3 oz (90 g) mushrooms, sliced
10 oz (300 g) beef fillet, cut into thin slices
¼ teaspoon cayenne pepper
salt and freshly ground pepper
½ cup (4 fl oz/125 ml) sour cream
½ cup (4 fl oz/125 ml) beef stock
8 oz (250 g) thick noodles, cooked, drained and
    buttered, to serve
1 tablespoon chopped fresh parsley, to serve

Heat 2 teaspoons oil in frying pan over medium heat. Add onion and mushrooms and cook, partially covered, 3 to 4 minutes. Set aside.

Heat remaining oil over high heat and cook beef for 1 to 2 minutes, stirring. Season with cayenne, salt and pepper.

Add mushroom mixture, sour cream and stock to beef and place over low heat until heated through, 1 to 2 minutes.

Serve stroganoff over noodles, sprinkled with parsley.

Tips

• Beef fillet is the best cut, as it does not need much cooking to become tender.

• If stock is unavailable, you can use water but the flavor won't be quite so good.

Best burgers

Preparation: 10 minutes

Cooking time: 15 minutes

Serves: 4

1¼ lb (625 g) lean ground (minced) beef

2 oz (60 g) fresh white breadcrumbs

2 oz (60 g) pitted (stoned) black olives, finely
  chopped

salt and freshly ground black pepper

1 red (Spanish) onion, sliced

1 clove garlic, crushed

1 tablespoon olive oil

4 tablespoons sun-dried tomato paste

10 oz (300 g) jar artichoke hearts in oil, drained

1 teaspoon pizza herbs (mixed herbs)

4 oz (125 g) fontina cheese, sliced

sesame-topped bread rolls, to serve

sprigs fresh basil, to serve

Preheat broiler (grill) to high.

Mix together beef, breadcrumbs, olives, salt and pepper. Shape mixture into four large, flat burgers. Broil (grill) burgers for 3 to 4 minutes each side.

Meanwhile, heat oil in frying pan and sauté onion and garlic until onion is soft. Spread each burger with 1 tablespoon sun-dried tomato paste. Arrange artichokes and onion on top, sprinkle with herbs and place cheese on top.

Return to broiler and cook until cheese has melted and vegetables have heated through. Serve on bread rolls garnished with fresh basil.

Braised chops

Preparation: 5 minutes

Cooking time: 25–40 minutes

Serves: 4

1¼–1½ lb (625–750 g) lamb, veal or pork chops

freshly ground black pepper

2 tablespoon vegetable or olive oil or butter

1 small onion

1 small stalk celery

¾ cup (6 fl oz/180 ml) liquid (see Tips)

½ teaspoon dried herb such as thyme, sage,
   rosemary

1 tablespoon cornstarch (cornflour)

2 tablespoons cold water

salt

2–3 tablespoons chopped parsley, to serve

Preheat oven to lowest temperature.

Trim excess fat from chops. Slash remaining fat almost through to meat in several places, to prevent curling. Sprinkle with pepper to taste.

Heat oil in a large, heavy-based frying pan over medium heat. Add chops and cook for 2 to 3 minutes each side, or until brown. Transfer chops to a plate and keep warm. Drain excess fat from pan, leaving 1 to 2 tablespoons fat with cooking juices.

Peel and chop onion and thinly slice celery. Add to pan and cook over medium heat, stirring, for 5 minutes or until golden. Add liquid and herb to pan and bring to a boil. Return chops to pan, reduce heat, cover and simmer gently for 20 to 25 minutes, or until tender, turning chops once. Less tender cuts may take 5 to 10 minutes more. Transfer chops to heated serving plate and keep warm in oven.

Mix cornstarch and water until blended. Add to cooking juices. Cook, stirring constantly, until sauce boils and thickens. Season to taste with salt and pepper. Pour sauce over chops, sprinkle with parsley and serve immediately.

Tips

• For best results, the chops should be about ¾ to 1 inch (2 to 2.5 cm) thick.

• For liquid, use water, stock, dry white or red wine, unsweetened fruit juice (e.g. orange or pineapple or apricot nectar), or undrained crushed canned tomatoes.

• Chopped scallions (shallots/spring onions), sliced leek or garlic, sliced button mushrooms or finely diced carrots can be added with the onion.

Chili con carne

Preparation: 5 minutes
Cooking time: 35–45 minutes
Serves: 4

½ stick celery
1 onion
1 clove garlic
1 green bell pepper (capsicum), halved and seeded
2 tablespoons olive or vegetable oil
12 oz (375 g) lean ground (minced) beef
2 x 14 oz (440 g) cans crushed tomatoes
2 tablespoons tomato paste
3 tablespoons chopped fresh oregano or 1 tablespoon
  dried
1½ tablespoons ground cumin
2 teaspoons Mexican-style chili powder
pinch of sugar
salt and freshly ground black pepper
14 oz (440 g) canned red kidney beans
rice or elbow macaroni, cooked

Trim coarse ends from celery and finely chop. Peel and finely chop onion and garlic. Cut bell pepper into ½-inch (1-cm) squares.

Heat oil in a large, heavy-based saucepan over medium heat and cook celery, onion, garlic and bell pepper, stirring for 5 minutes, or until golden.

Crumble beef into pan and cook until brown, stirring to break up lumps.

Add undrained, crushed tomatoes, tomato paste, oregano, cumin, chili powder, sugar and pepper. Bring to a boil. Reduce heat and simmer gently, stirring occasionally, for 20 to 30 minutes.

Rinse red kidney beans and add to sauce. Cook for a further 10 minutes, or until sauce thickens. Serve over cooked rice or elbow macaroni.

Garlic pork and chive dumplings

Preparation: 20 minutes

Cooking time: 20 minutes

Serves: 4–6

1 pack (20–24) won ton skins (wrappers)

5 dried mushrooms

18 oz (560 g) coarsely minced (ground) pork

2 oz (60 g) bamboo shoots, drained and finely
  chopped

³/₄ cup loosely packed chopped garlic chives

2 tablespoons light soy sauce

1 teaspoon sugar

salt and white pepper

cornstarch (cornflour)

vegetable oil

Defrost won ton skins, if frozen, under a cloth to prevent
them drying out.

Drain the mushrooms and remove stems. Chop caps
finely. Combine with the pork, bamboo shoots, garlic
chives and seasonings.

Place a portion of the filling in the center of each skin
and bring the corners in together to form square
parcels.

In a small saucepan make a paste of cornstarch and
water, boiling it until it becomes translucent. Use this to
seal the dumplings.

Place dumplings in a steamer and steam for 15 minutes.
Remove and set aside for 10 minutes to allow the skins
to dry.

Heat a nonstick pan and add a film of oil. Fry the
dumplings briefly on both sides. Serve with a hot chili
sauce.

Greek-style kebabs

Preparation: 10 minutes plus 30 minutes marinating
Cooking time: 5 minutes
Serves: 4

½ cup (4 fl oz/125 ml) extra virgin Greek olive oil
juice of 1 lemon
1 tablespoon chopped fresh oregano
1 tablespoon chopped fresh thyme
salt and freshly ground black pepper
1⅓ lb (560 g) rump steak, cut into 16 cubes
12 oz (375 g) halloumi cheese cut into 12 cubes
12 cherry tomatoes

Mix together olive oil, lemon juice, oregano, thyme, and salt and pepper in a ceramic or glass bowl. Add cubed steak and cheese and mix well. Cover and chill for at least 30 minutes, or overnight.

Remove meat and cheese from bowl, reserving marinade.

Preheat broiler (grill) to high. Divide meat, cheese and tomatoes among eight kebab skewers, beginning and ending with steak. Broil (grill) or barbecue for about 5 minutes, turning and brushing with marinade from time to time.

Serve immediately.

Irish lamb pot

Preparation: 10–15 minutes
Cooking time: 1 ¼–1 1½ hours
Serves: 4

1½ lb (750 g) boneless lean lamb
2 tablespoons all-purpose (plain) flour
salt and freshly ground black pepper
2 tablespoons vegetable or olive oil
1 oz (30 g) butter
1 large onion, peeled and chopped
4 oz (125 g) bacon, chopped
2 cups (16 fl oz/500 ml) beef stock
2 carrots, peeled and thickly sliced
8 small onions, peeled and halved
6 oz (180 g) button mushrooms, halved
½ cup (2 oz/60 g) frozen peas
1 teaspoon dried thyme or majoram
cooked rice, pasta or couscous, to serve

Use a sharp knife to trim excess fat from meat. Cut into
1-inch (2.5-cm) cubes.

Place flour and salt and pepper to taste in a plastic bag.
Add meat, seal and shake until cubes are evenly coated.

Heat oil and butter in a deep, heavy-based frying pan over
medium heat until foaming subsides. Add meat in batches
and cook, turning frequently, until brown on all sides. Use
a slotted spoon to transfer cooked meat to a plate.

Add onion and bacon to pan and cook, stirring, over
medium heat for 5 minutes, or until soft. Return meat to
pan with stock, vegetables and thyme and bring to a boil,
stirring. Reduce heat, partially cover and simmer for
1 hour, or until meat is almost tender and sauce thickens
slightly, stirring occasionally.

Serve with cooked rice, pasta or couscous.

Korean beef and vegetable steamboat

Preparation: 20 minutes

Cooking time: 25 minutes

Serves: 4–6

1 lb (500 g) daikon (mooli) radish, peeled and diced

salt

1 onion, chopped

1 clove garlic, chopped

1 tablespoon sesame oil

1 tablespoon sesame seeds

12 oz (375 g) lean ground (minced) beef

1 tablespoon soy sauce

1/2 teaspoon paprika

1/4 teaspoon cayenne pepper

1 egg, beaten

1 tablespoon sunflower oil

2 medium zucchini (courgettes), ends removed and thinly sliced

bunch scallions (shallots/spring onions), chopped

4 oz (125 g) mushrooms, sliced

8 oz (250 g) can bamboo shoots, drained

12 oz (375 g) lean steak, cut into very thin strips

8 oz (250g) bean curd (tofu), diced

4 cups (32 fl oz/1 L) Korean soup base or beef stock

1 red chili, seeded and chopped

Korean sticky rice and kim chee (Korean pickled cabbage), to serve

Cook daikon in lightly salted water for 10 minutes and drain.

Heat sesame oil in a frying pan and cook onion and garlic for 2 to 3 minutes, until onion is soft. Mix daikon with onion and sesame seeds.

In a bowl, mix beef with soy sauce, paprika, cayenne and egg and form into 16 to 20 balls. Heat sunflower oil in a wok or frying pan and fry meatballs for about 10 minutes, until brown and cooked through.

Mix together zucchini, onions, mushrooms and bamboo shoots.

In a Korean steamboat or a large fondue pan set over a burner, layer half the daikon, half the steak, half the vegetables, half the bean curd and half the meatballs, then repeat the layering. Put soup base and chili into a pan, bring to a boil, and pour over meat and vegetables. Simmer at the table for about 5 minutes, until steak is cooked and vegetables are heated through.

Serve with bowls of Korean sticky rice and kim chee.

Tip

The steamboat can also be cooked in a similar manner on the stove in a heavy metal casserole dish that can be brought to the table.

Lamb with creamy cannellini beans

Preparation: 5 minutes

Cooking time: 20 minutes

Serves: 2

2 teaspoons olive oil

1 clove garlic, minced

2 thin slices pancetta, cut into strips

1 can (14 oz/440 g) cannellini beans, rinsed and drained

6 fresh sage leaves or ½ teaspoon dried

2 teaspoons fresh thyme leaves or 1 teaspoon dried

salt and freshly ground pepper

¼ cup (2 fl oz/60 ml) light (single) cream

10 oz (300 g) trimmed lamb chops (cutlets)

¼ cup (1 oz/30 g) shaved parmesan, to serve

Heat oil in frying pan over medium heat. Add garlic and pancetta and cook, 2 to 3 minutes. Add beans and cook 2 to 3 more minutes. Add herbs, salt, pepper and cream and heat through, about 2 minutes.

Meanwhile, chargrill or broil (grill) lamb for 4 to 5 minutes on each side for medium.

Serve lamb with beans sprinkled with parmesan.

Tip

Instead of lamb, try grilled tuna steaks—cook them 3 minutes on each side for medium-rare.

Meatballs in chunky tomato sauce with spaghetti

Preparation: 10 minutes

Cooking time: 20 minutes

Serves: 4

1 tablespoon olive oil

1 large onion, finely chopped

1 small hot red chili, finely chopped

2 cloves garlic, pressed (crushed)

1 medium-size (7 oz/220 g) waxy potato, finely diced

1 tablespoon chopped fresh basil

2 tablespoons chopped fresh oregano

2 tablespoons white wine

1 (14 oz/440 g) can tomatoes, coarsely chopped

1 lb (500 g) ground (minced) beef

2 cloves garlic, pressed (crushed)

2 tablespoons chopped fresh basil

1 tablespoon chopped fresh oregano

1 egg, lightly beaten

2 tablespoons olive oil

1 lb (500 g) spaghetti, cooked and drained, to serve

Heat oil in a large frying pan. Add onion and sauté until tender. Stir in chili, garlic and potato and cook over medium heat, stirring constantly, until garlic is fragrant and slightly golden, about 3 minutes.

Stir in herbs, wine and tomatoes and cook, covered, over low heat, stirring occasionally, for 10 minutes, or until potato is tender.

Meanwhile, combine meat, garlic, herbs and egg in a bowl and mix well. Roll into 1-inch (2.5-cm) balls. Heat oil in frying pan and fry meatballs in batches over medium heat for 3 minutes or until lightly browned and cooked through.

Toss meatballs into tomato sauce and stir over low heat 2 minutes, or until heated through. Serve with hot spaghetti.

Mediterranean beef stir-fry with warm vinaigrette

Preparation: 10 minutes

Cooking time: 15 minutes

Serves: 4

2 tablespoons olive oil

13 oz (400 g) beef tenderloin, thinly sliced

2 medium zucchini (courgettes), sliced

1 medium onion, sliced

4 large mushrooms, sliced

5 oz (150 g) snow peas (mange tout), halved

1 medium-size red bell pepper (capsicum), seeded
   and sliced

6 scallions (spring onions/shallots), sliced

2 tablespoons additional olive oil

2 tablespoons red wine vinegar

1 tablespoon chopped fresh thyme

1 teaspoon sugar

1 teaspoon cracked black peppercorns

cooked couscous, to serve

Heat 1 tablespoon oil in a large frying pan or wok over high heat. Add beef and stir-fry until lightly browned. Remove from pan.

Add 1 tablespoon oil to pan. Stir in zucchini, onion, mushrooms, snow peas, bell pepper and scallions and stir-fry until vegetables are heated through but still crisp, about 10 minutes.

Stir in beef until heated through, about 2 minutes.

Combine additional oil, vinegar, thyme, sugar and peppercorns in a small bowl and beat with a fork until well combined. Pour mixture into pan and cook, stirring, for 1 more minute. Serve stir-fry on bed of couscous.

Mediterranean-style steaks

Preparation: 5 minutes

Cooking time: 10 minutes

Serves: 4

4 beef sirloin, round or fillet steaks, 8 oz (250 g) each

2 cloves garlic, minced

2 tablespoons Dijon, seeded or mild English mustard

2 tablespoons olive oil

1 medium-size red bell pepper (capsicum), thinly sliced

2 medium onions, sliced

2 tablespoons red wine

1 tablespoon finely chopped fresh oregano or

2 teaspoons dried

Rub steaks with garlic and spread with mustard. Heat 1 tablespoon oil in large frying pan. Add steaks and cook over medium heat for 3 minutes on one side.

Add remaining oil, bell pepper and onion. Turn steaks and cook 2 more minutes.

Add wine and oregano to pan and cook, stirring, until bell pepper is tender, about 2 minutes longer. Serve steaks topped with bell pepper, onion and pan juices.

Tips

• Serve with baked potatoes or crunchy potato wedges.

• Fresh or dried marjoram makes a good alternative to oregano.

• Sprinkle a tablespoon of chopped chives over the steaks before serving.

Minted couscous salad with lamb and caramelized onions

Preparation: 10 minutes

Cooking time: 35 minutes

Serves: 2

1 cup (6½ oz/200 g) couscous

2 cups (16 fl oz/500 ml) boiling water

2 tablespoons butter

salt and freshly ground pepper

½ cup (1 oz/30 g) chopped fresh mint

1 small cucumber, finely chopped

1 tomato, diced

2 teaspoons grated lemon zest

2 tablespoons olive oil

2 onions, sliced

10 oz (300 g) lamb fillets

Place couscous in a bowl and pour boiling water over. Cover and let stand 5 minutes. Fluff witha fork, adding 1 tablespoon butter, and salt and pepper to taste. Add mint, cucumber, tomato and lemon zest and set aside.

Heat 1 tablespoon oil and remaining butter in a shallow pan with a lid. Add onions and cook, over medium heat, partially covered, for 5 minutes. Uncover and cook until onions are golden and slightly caramelized, about 10 more minutes.

Heat remaining oil on a barbecue or stovetop grill or in a heavy-based frying pan over high heat and cook lamb fillets for 3 to 4 minutes on each side for medium-rare. Let rest for 5 minutes before slicing.

Toss couscous and serve with lamb and caramelized onions.

Tips

• Coriander (cilantro) leaves or basil is good instead of mint.

• If preferred, serve with chicken or firm white-fleshed fish fillets such as snapper.

Moroccan-style lamb

Preparation: 10 minutes

Cooking time: 15 minutes

Serves: 4

12 lamb chops (cutlets)

1 teaspoon ground coriander

1 teaspoon ground cinnamon

1 teaspoon ground cumin

3 tablespoons chopped fresh parsley

2 tablespoons honey

1¼ cups (8 oz/250 g) couscous

1 tablespoon butter

2 tomatoes, chopped

1 hothouse (continental) cucumber, seeded and
   chopped

1 teaspoon paprika

3 tablespoons vegetable oil

Trim fat from lamb. Combine coriander, cinnamon,
cumin, 1 tablespoon parsley and honey in medium bowl.
Add lamb and coat with mixture on all sides.

Combine couscous and butter in medium bowl. Pour
1 cup (8 fl oz/250 ml) boiling water over couscous and
stir briefly to combine. Cover with plastic wrap for
3 minutes, then gently stir with fork until grains are
separated and lightly fluffed. Let cool.

Stir tomatoes, cucumber, remaining 2 tablespoons
parsley and paprika into fluffed couscous and set aside.

Heat oil in frying pan and brown marinated lamb in
batches, 2 minutes on each side. Serve lamb on bed of
couscous salad.

Tips

- This lamb is best cooked medium-rare, but if you
  prefer, it can be cooked longer.

- Chicken thighs make a good alternative—use eight
  trimmed thigh fillets.

- When buying couscous, make sure you choose the
  precooked variety.

- If hothouse cucumbers are unavailable, any small
  cucumber will suffice.

Panfried lamb with bean salad and gremolata

Preparation: 10 minutes

Cooking time: 15 minutes

Serves: 2

½ cup (2 oz/60 g) fresh broad beans or sliced green
   beans

1 can (14 oz/440 g) cannellini beans, rinsed and
   drained

1 tablespoon lemon juice

2 tablespoons olive oil

1 large ripe tomato, chopped

1 small purple onion, diced

2 teaspoons olive oil

10 oz (300 g) lamb fillet or leg steaks

2 teaspoons grated lemon zest

1 tablespoon chopped fresh parsley

1 clove garlic, pressed (crushed)

Cook broad beans in boiling water until just tender, 2 to
3 minutes.

Combine with drained cannellini beans, lemon juice,
olive oil, tomato and onion. Set aside.

Heat oil in frying pan and cook lamb over medium-high
heat for 4 to 5 minutes on each side. Remove and let
stand for 5 minutes.

Slice warm lamb and arrange over bean salad. Combine
lemon zest, parsley and garlic, sprinkle over and serve.

Tips

• Gremolata is a mixture of grated lemon zest, finely
  chopped parsley and pressed garlic.

• Use any green beans or peas for the salad.

• Any canned beans will work as a substitute for
  cannellini beans.

Perfectly cooked steaks

Preparation: 1–2 minutes

Cooking time: 10–12 minutes

Serves: 4

4 x 6–8 oz (180–250 g) steaks e.g. T-bone, sirloin,
  porterhouse, rib-eye (scotch) fillet, New York strip,
  (pictured) cut 1 inch (2.5 cm) thick

vegetable or olive oil

freshly ground black pepper

Heat barbecue until coals are ash-covered and glowing, or preheat a broiler (grill) to medium-high. Place cooking rack about 4 inches (10 cm) away from heat.

Trim excess fat from steaks and sprinkle with black pepper to taste. Brush rack with oil to prevent meat sticking.

Cook steaks for 30 to 45 seconds each side. Reduce heat slightly (or move steaks from hot part of barbecue) and cook, turning once only, for 4 to 5 minutes each side, or until cooked as desired. Serve immediately.

Tips

• Whether barbecued or broiled (grilled), the rule is the same: sear meat quickly on both sides to seal in juices, then reduce heat and cook as desired. This also applies to chops, whether lamb, pork or veal.

• To test if cooked: press the meat with tongs—never cut or pierce with a knife or fork, as juices will run and meat will be dry. Rare steak feels soft and red juices puddle on the surface; medium is firm but pliable and juices are still pink; well-done is firm, stiff and dry-looking.

• Your can marinate steak for 30 to 60 minutes at room temperature in ½ cup (4 fl oz/125 ml) beer, 1 clove garlic (peeled and finely chopped), and 1 tablespoon each hot English mustard and honey. Drain steaks, reserving marinade, and pat dry with paper towel. Cook, basting once or twice with marinade.

• Rub steak with olive oil and sprinkle with crumbled dried rosemary, thyme, oregano or sage leaves.

• Serve steaks with a savory butter. Beat 4 oz (125 g) soft butter until creamy with one or more of the following: 1 to 2 tablespoons hot English mustard, horseradish relish or chili sauce; 2 to 3 teaspoons grated lemon rind; 2 peeled and finely chopped garlic cloves; 2 to 3 tablespoons chopped fresh herb (or 1 to 2 teaspoons dried), such as mint, basil, sage, rosemary, dill, chives, or a combination.

Pesto sauce on grilled lamb

Preparation: 5 minutes

Cooking time: 10–12 minutes

Serves:

2 large cloves garlic, crushed

pinch salt

2 tablespoons pine nuts

2 cups fresh basil leaves

2 oz (60 g) parmesan, grated

5 tablespoons extra virgin olive oil

4 x 6–8 oz (180–250 g) lamb cutlets

vegetable or olive oil

freshly ground black pepper

Mash garlic with salt in a small bowl.

Process pine nuts, basil and parmesan in a blender or food processor with 1 tablespoon olive oil. Add garlic. With motor running, pour in remaining oil in a steady stream so the pesto becomes a smooth paste.

Heat barbecue until coals are ash-covered and glowing, or preheat a broiler (grill) to medium-high. Place cooking rack about 4 inch (10 cm) away from heat.

Trim excess fat from lamb and sprinkle with black pepper to taste. Brush rack with oil to prevent meat sticking.

Cook lamb for 30 to 45 seconds each side. Reduce heat slightly (or move lamb from hot part of barbecue) and cook, turning once only, for 4 to 5 minutes each side, or until cooked as desired.

Serve immediately with pesto sauce.

Tips

- Try toasting the pine nuts first. Spread them out on a baking tray and place in a medium oven or under the broiler (grill). Shake the tray every minute or two to ensure even cooking—be careful they don't burn.

- Instead of parmesan, use another hard Italian cheese, such as pecorino.

Pork cutlets pané with sauce piquante

Preparation: 15 minutes

Cooking time: 10 minutes

Serves: 4

8 slices pork cutlets, ½ inch (1 cm) thick

1 tablespoon Cajun spice mix (see page 128—Cajun fried chicken strips)

1 cup (4 oz/125 g) all-purpose (plain) flour

2 eggs

1 teaspoon dried marjoram

1 teaspoon salt

¼ teaspoon black pepper

1 cup (4 oz/125 g) fine cracker crumbs or dry breadcrumbs

1 quantity of sauce piquante (see Tips)

¾ cup (6 fl oz/180 ml) vegetable oil

Trim fat from the pork or veal cutlets and flatten them slightly with the side of a cleaver. Slash edges in two or three places so they won't curl up when frying.

Using three pie plates or flat bowls, blend the spice mix and flour in one; beat the eggs with 1 teaspoon water in another; and mix the majoram, salt, pepper and crumbs in the third (omit salt if using salted crackers for crumbs). Heat the sauce piquante in a saucepan and keep warm.

Heat the oil to 350°F (180°C) in a large frying pan. Dip both sides of each cutlet first in the seasoned flour, then in the egg and then in the crumbs. Fry the hot oil for 3 to 5 minutes on each side or until brown and crisp. Drain on paper towel. Serve with sauce piquante spooned over cutlets.

Tips

• To make sauce piquante: heat ¼ cup (2 fl oz/60 ml) olive or vegetable oil in a saucepan over medium heat and sauté 1 finely chopped medium onion; 6 finely chopped cloves garlic; ½ green and ½ red bell pepper (capsicum), finely chopped; and 1 or 2 seeded and finely chopped hot fresh chilies, to taste. Stir occasionally, until onion is soft and translucent, about 3 to 5 minutes. Add 3 cups (24 fl oz/750 ml) chopped fresh tomatoes (or canned Italian-style tomatoes) with juice; 1 teaspoon each of dried thyme and dried majoram; 2 bay leaves, 2 tablespoon Cajun spice mix (see above); ¼ teaspoon cayenne pepper; 2 tablespoons red wine vinegar; 1 tablespoon Worcestershire sauce; ¾ teaspoon or more, to taste, Tabasco or other hot pepper sauce; 1 teaspoon or more, to taste, salt; and ¼ teaspoon black pepper. Cook for 10 to 15 minutes, or until slightly thickened.

• You may be able to buy sauce piquante from the supermarket.

Pork fillets with creamy dill potatoes and apple sauce

Preparation: 5 minutes

Cooking time: 30 minutes

Serves: 2

7 oz (220 g) new potatoes, halved

½ cup (4 fl oz/125 ml) chicken stock

¼ cup (2 fl oz/60 ml) sour cream

1 tablespoon chopped fresh dill or flat-leaf parsley

salt and freshly ground pepper

2 teaspoons olive oil

10 oz (300 g) pork fillet

1 large green apple, cored and thinly sliced

2 tablespoons water

2 tablespoons superfine (caster) sugar

2 teaspoons white wine vinegar

Cook potatoes in boiling water until tender. Drain and set aside.

Bring chicken stock to boil; remove from heat. Add cooked potatoes and let cool slightly. Stir in sour cream and dill. Season to taste.

Heat oil in frying pan over medium-high heat. Add pork and cook, for about 10 minutes, turning. Set aside.

Meanwhile, combine apple, water, sugar and vinegar in small saucepan and bring to a boil. Simmer until apples are soft, about 10 minutes, stirring.

Serve sliced pork with potatoes and apple sauce.

Sausages with mashed hummus potatoes

Preparation: 5 minutes

Cooking time: 10 minutes

Serves: 4

2 cloves garlic, crushed

1 teaspoon salt

1½ tablespoons tahini (sesame paste)

juice of 1–2 lemons

5 oz (150 g) canned chickpeas (garbanzo beans), drained

1 lb (500 g) potatoes, peeled and cut into quarters

2 tablespoons hot milk

1 teaspoon butter

salt and pepper, to taste

8 sausages

green salad, to serve

Mash garlic with salt in small bowl. Blend with tahini and lemon juice in a blender or food processor. Add chickpeas and puree until smooth.

Place potatoes in enough cold salted water to cover. Bring to a boil and cook, covered, until potatoes are tender, about 20 to 30 minutes. Test with a skewer.

Meanwhile, prick sausages with a fork and place under a preheated broiler (grill). Cook, turning, until browned and cooked through, about 10 to 15 minutes.

Drain potatoes, then return to the hot saucepan and leave for a couple of minutes until extra moisture evaporates, shaking occasionally. Add milk, butter, salt and pepper and a generous portion of hummus, and mash with a fork until smooth. Then beat with a wooden spoon to make extra creamy.

Serve sausages with hummus potatoes and green salad.

Tip

Hummus keeps well and makes an interesting base for bread and pizzas. It teams beautifully with either tomato, roasted bell pepper (capsicum) or eggplant (aubergine), or a combination of these. It also lifts a salad sandwich.

Sesame lamb

Preparation: 20 minutes plus 30 minutes marinating
Cooking time: 15 minutes
Serves: 4

1½ lb (750 g) lean lamb
3–4 cloves garlic, finely chopped
2 tablespoons yellow rice wine or sake
2½ tablespoons sesame oil
1 tablespoon dark soy sauce
1 tablespoon light soy sauce
3 teaspoons sugar
2 teaspoons cornstarch (cornflour)
2 tablespoons vegetable oil
1 large onion, finely sliced
cooked white rice, to serve
1 tablespoon white sesame seeds, toasted, to serve
2 scallions (shallots/spring onion) tops, shredded, to
    serve
1 fresh red chili, seeded and shredded, to serve

Cut the lamb into thin slices, stack several slices together at a time and slice crosswise into very fine shreds. Place in a dish and add the garlic, wine, sesame oil, soy sauces, sugar and cornstarch. Mix well and marinate for at least 30 minutes.

Heat a tabletop or electric frying pan and add the oil. Sauté the onion until lightly browned, then push to the side of the pan. Add the meat, retaining any excess marinade, and cook on a very high heat, stirring and turning continually until the meat is well cooked and very aromatic. Stir in the onions and any remaining marinade. Turn off the heat.

The dish can be served directly from the pan into bowls of steamed white rice and garnished with the sesame seeds, scallions and chili.

Singapore noodles

THE HENLEY COLLEGE LIBRARY

Preparation: 15 minutes

Cooking time: 10 minutes

Serves: 4

9 oz (270 g) rice stick noodles

7 oz (220 g) broccoli, cut into small florets

4 oz (125 g) thin asparagus spears

salt

2 tablespoons sunflower oil

1 lb (500 g) top rump steak, cut into long thin strips

4 oz (125 g) bean sprouts

1 lb (500 g) pak choi (Chinese broccoli), thick stems removed

2 tablespoons sesame oil

3 tablespoons soy sauce

3 tablespoons sweet chili sauce

Put noodles into a large saucepan and cover with boiling water. Bring back to a boil, remove from heat and let stand for 8 to 10 minutes, until tender.

Blanch broccoli and asparagus in lightly salted boiling water for 2 minutes; drain well.

Heat sunflower oil in a large frying pan or wok. Stir-fry the beef for 2 to 3 minutes, until brown. Add broccoli, asparagus, bean sprouts and pak choi and stir-fry for a further 2 to 3 minutes, until heated through.

Strain noodles, rinse with boiling water and drain well. Add to the frying pan. Mix well, then stir in sesame oil, soy and chili sauce.

Transfer to a warm serving dish and serve immediately.

Southern-style meatloaf

Preparation: 10 minutes

Cooking time: 45 minutes

Serves: 4

1 tablespoon vegetable oil

1 large onion, finely chopped

1 celery stalk, finely chopped

½ red bell pepper (capsicum), finely chopped

4 tablespoons tomato ketchup

1 lb (500 g) lean ground (minced) beef

½ lb (250 g) lean ground (minced) pork

2 tablespoons Worcestershire sauce

2 teaspoons ground coriander

½ to 2 teaspoons Tabasco or other hot pepper sauce,
  or to taste

2 cups (4 oz/125 g) fresh white breadcrumbs

2 eggs, lightly beaten

2 tablespoons chopped fresh cilantro (coriander)
  leaves

2 small fresh red chilies, chopped (optional)

Heat oven to 350°F (180°C/Gas 4). Heat oil in frying pan
over medium heat. Add onion, celery and bell pepper and
cook, stirring, until soft.

Mix onion mixture, ½ of the ketchup and remaining
ingredients in large bowl until well combined. Spread
mixture evenly in lightly greased 9-inch (22-cm) pie dish.
Spread with remaining ketchup. Bake for 30 minutes; if
meatloaf looks as if it is drying out, cover with foil after
15 minutes. Let stand for 5 minutes before serving.

Steak sandwiches with cream cheese and red pepper spread

Preparation: 5 minutes

Cooking time: 20 minutes

Serves: 2

1 tablespoon butter

2 teaspoons olive oil

1 onion, thinly sliced

½ red bell pepper (capsicum), seeded and thinly
  sliced

1 teaspoon balsamic vinegar

2 teaspoons shredded fresh basil (optional)

salt and freshly ground pepper

2 to 4 club steaks or minute steaks (8 to 10 oz/
  250 to 300 g)

½ red bell pepper (capsicum), roastedthen seeded
  and peeled

3 tablespoons soft cream cheese

2 teaspoons butter

½ teaspoon paprika

½ teaspoon crushed caraway seeds (optional)

slices of thick Italian-style bread, to serve

sliced tomato and arugula (rocket), to serve

Heat butter and oil in frying pan over medium heat. Add onion and bell pepper and cook for 7 to 10 minutes. Add vinegar and cook for another 2 to 3 minutes. Stir in basil and season with salt and pepper. Remove mixture from pan and set aside.

Add steaks to pan and cook over high heat for 1 minute on each side.

For spread, combine bell pepper, cream cheese, butter, paprika, and caraway seeds in blender or food processor and blend until smooth.

Spread bread with cream cheese mixture, then fill sandwiches with steaks, tomato and arugula.

Tips

• The number of steaks will depend on their size. Make sure they are thin; if not, gently pound them.

• Cook steaks for an extra minute if you prefer them well cooked.

Steak with garlic butter and red pepper relish

Preparation: 5 minutes

Cooking time: 20 minutes

Serves: 2

2 cloves garlic, pressed (crushed)

1 anchovy fillet (optional)

3 tablespoons butter, softened

1 tablespoon olive oil

1 red bell pepper (capsicum), seeded and thinly
   sliced

½ teaspoon balsamic vinegar

2 beef steaks (your choice of cut), about 9 to 13 oz
   (270 to 400 g)

For garlic butter, stir garlic and anchovy into softened butter. Pat into small dish and refrigerate until ready to serve.

To prepare relish, heat oil in frying pan over medium-low heat. Add pepper and cook, partially covered, for 10 minutes. Stir in vinegar and cook for 10 more minutes, uncovered.

Broil (grill) steak until cooked as desired. Serve with garlic butter and relish.

Serve with baked potatoes and salad.

Steak with Mediterranean vegetables and aioli

Preparation: 10 minutes

Cooking time: 25 minutes

Serves: 2

¼ cup (2 fl oz/60 ml) whole-egg mayonnaise

2 tablespoons sour cream or crème fraîche

2 cloves garlic, pressed (crushed)

1 teaspoon finely grated lemon zest

1 small eggplant (aubergine), thinly sliced

2 plum (egg) tomatoes, halved

1 small purple onion, quartered

½ red bell pepper (capsicum)

2 tablespoons olive oil

1 lb (500 g) sirloin steak, 1¼ inch (3 cm) thick

1 tablespoon lemon juice

salt and freshly ground pepper

basil leaves, to serve

Combine mayonnaise, sour cream, garlic and lemon zest to make aioli and let stand.

Brush eggplant slices, tomato halves, onion quarters and whole bell pepper with olive oil and place on baking sheet. Broil (grill) for 10 to 15 minutes, turning eggplant, onion and bell pepper after 5 to 7 minutes. Set aside.

Broil (grill) steak at medium-high heat for 7 to 10 minutes on each side for medium, brushing with a little lemon juice while cooking. Season with salt and pepper.

Peel, seed and slice roasted bell pepper.

Serve steak with vegetables and aïoli.

Tips

• Everything can be cooked under the same broiler or on the same grill.

• A spoonful of pesto and a handful of black olives make a colorful accompaniment.

Sukiyaki

Preparation: 10 minutes

Cooking time: 10 minutes

Serves: 4

2 tablespoons mirin (Japanese sweet sake)

2 tablespoons sake

2 tablespoons soy sauce

1 tablespoon instant dashi powder

1 teaspoon brown sugar

1 cup (8 fl oz/250 ml) water

4 tablespoons sunflower oil, for frying

1¼ lb (625 g) fillet steak, cut into paper thin slices

4 oz (125 g) shiitake mushrooms

6 oz (180 g) young leeks, thinly sliced diagonally

6 oz (180 g) Chinese (celery) cabbage, shredded

7 oz (220 g) bean sprouts

8 oz (250 g) bean curd (tofu), diced

7 oz (220 g) cooked shirataki noodles

individual bowls of cooked Japanese rice, to serve

Mix together mirin, sake, soy sauce, dashi powder, sugar and water in a small pan, and bring to a boil. Transfer to a small jug and set aside.

Heat oil in a frying pan. Add the beef, vegetables, bean curd and noodles to pan and stir-fry quickly until meat is cooked. Transfer to a warmed serving dish and serve immediately with mirin sauce and rice.

Tip

Sukiyaki is traditionally cooked at the table in either an electric frying pan or a heavy frying pan set over a burner, with each guest cooking their individual portions. To do so, arrange beef, vegetables, tofu and noodles attractively on serving dishes and serve a bowl of rice for each individual. Heat 1 tablespoon oil in frying pan and add a quarter of the beef, stir-fry quickly and transfer to rice bowls. Then add a quarter of vegetables, tofu and noodles to the pan and cook quickly, moistening with a little sauce. Transfer to bowls. Repeat with remaining ingredients in a similar manner, as required.

Thai beef salad

Preparation: 10 minutes

Cooking time: 5 minutes

Serves: 2–4

1½ lb (750 g) sirloin (boneless rump) steak

4 tablespoons lime juice

4 tablespoons fish sauce (nam pla)

2 chilies, seeded and finely chopped

1 clove garlic, finely chopped

approx. 1-inch (2-cm) piece ginger, peeled and
    grated

1 teaspoon palm sugar or brown sugar

½ lettuce, preferably cos

1 large purple onion

1 small hothouse (continental) cucumber

2–4 tablespoons fresh basil or mint, chopped

2–4 tablespoons fresh cilantro (coriander) leaves,
    chopped

Sear steak in a hot frying pan or under broiler (grill) for a few minutes each side , until cooked; try to leave it pink in the middle.

Meanwhile, combine lime juice, fish sauce, chilies, garlic, ginger and sugar and set aside.

Remove meat from heat and let rest by placing it on a cool surface (such as a plate or chopping board).

Tear lettuce into pieces, cut onion into thin wedges, slice cucumber into thin strips. Arrange in large bowl.

Add basil and cilantro to dressing and pour over salad.

Slice meat into very thin strips. Add to salad, toss, and serve.

Tips

- You can stir-fry steak in a little sesame oil in a wok if preferred.

- Slices of scallion (shallots/spring onions) or white onion can be substituted for purple onion.

Two salsas with beef fajitas

Preparation: 25 minutes

Cooking time: 10 minutes

Serves: 4

Three-tomato salsa

1 teaspoon crushed coriander seeds

1 small red (Spanish) onion, chopped

2 medium red tomatoes, diced

2 medium yellow tomatoes, diced

4 oz (125 g) sun-dried tomatoes in oil, drained and
  chopped

1 tablespoon oil from sun-dried tomato jar

1–2 teaspoons jalapeño pepper sauce

1 tablespoon chopped fresh cilantro (coriander)
  leaves

Avocado salsa

1 ripe avocado

2 tablespoons low-fat sour cream

1 clove garlic, pressed (crushed)

1 tablespoon lime juice

2–3 drops Tabasco sauce

salt and freshly ground black pepper

grated zest of 1 lime

Beef fajitas

1 clove garlic, sliced

1 large onion, sliced

1 large red bell pepper (capsicum), seeded and
  sliced

1 large green bell pepper (capsicum), seeded and
  sliced

1 jalapeño pepper, chopped, or 1 teaspoon hot chili
  sauce

2 tablespoons olive oil

1½ lb (700 g) rib-eye or rump steak, cut into thin
  strips

juice of 1 lime

flour tortillas, sour cream and shredded lettuce to
  serve

To make three-tomato salsa, combine coriander seeds, onion, tomatoes, oil, pepper sauce and cilantro in a bowl. Mix well and transfer to a serving dish.

To make avocado salsa, mash avocado with sour cream. Stir in garlic, lime juice, Tabasco sauce, salt and pepper. Transfer to a serving dish and sprinkle lime rind over the top.

In a large frying pan or wok stir-fry garlic, onion, bell peppers, and jalapeño pepper and beef in oil for 2 to 3 minutes until beef is cooked through. Stir in lime juice, salt and pepper. Transfer to a warm serving dish and serve with flour tortillas, sour cream, shredded lettuce and the two salsas.

Veal with spinach and mozzarella

Preparation: 5 minutes

Cooking time: 20–25 minutes

Serves: 2

1 tablespoon butter

1 tablespoon olive oil

1/2 small purple onion, sliced

7 oz (220 g) fresh English spinach leaves

2 anchovy fillets

1 tablespoon dried currants

1 tablespoon chopped fresh parsley

10 oz (300 g) veal leg steaks

1/4 cup (2 fl oz/60 ml) white wine

salt and freshly ground pepper

5 oz (150 g) fresh mozzarella, sliced

Preheat oven to 350°F (180°C/Gas 4).

Heat butter and 2 teaspoons olive oil in ovenproof frying pan. Add onion and cook for 2 minutes over medium heat. Add spinach, anchovies and currants and cook until spinach has wilted, 2 to 3 more minutes. Stir in parsley. Remove from pan and set aside.

Heat remaining oil in pan over high heat and cook veal steaks for 2 minutes on each side. Pour wine over and cook over medium heat for 1 more minute.

Pile spinach mixture on each steak, season with salt and pepper and top with cheese slices. Bake 10 minutes or until cheese has melted, or broil (grill) at medium heat 3 to 4 minutes.

Tip

Instead of veal, you can use beef minute steaks or chicken breasts.

Veal steaks with sun-dried tomato salsa

Preparation: 10 minutes

Cooking time: 20 minutes

Serves: 2

2 ripe tomatoes, diced

2 sun-dried tomatoes, chopped

2 teaspoons oil from sun-dried tomatoes

1 teaspoon red wine vinegar

salt and freshly ground pepper

13 oz (400 g) potatoes

2 teaspoons chopped fresh rosemary or 1 teaspoon
   dried

salt and freshly ground pepper

2 tablespoons finely grated parmesan

1/2 cup (about 1 1/2 oz/45 g) fine dry breadcrumbs

2 to 4 veal leg steaks (about 10 to 13 oz/300 to
   400 g), gently pounded

1 egg, beaten

1 tablespoon olive oil

1/4 cup (2 fl oz/60 ml) light (single) cream

1 tablespoon butter

1 clove garlic, pressed (crushed)

For salsa, combine tomatoes, oil, vinegar and salt and pepper and let stand.

Boil potatoes until tender. Drain, return to pan and cover to keep warm.

Meanwhile, combine rosemary, salt and pepper, parmesan and breadcrumbs and spread over plate. Dip each veal steak on both sides in egg, then breadcrumb mixture.

Heat oil in frying pan over medium heat and cook veal for 3 to 4 minutes on each side.

Mash potatoes, stirring in cream, butter and garlic.

Spoon salsa over veal and serve with potatoes.

vegetables, eggs & nuts

Asparagus with poached egg and basil butter dressing

Preparation: 5 minutes

Cooking time: 15 minutes

Serves: 2

2 bunches asparagus, trimmed and cut into
  2-inch (5-cm) pieces

2 tablespoons butter

2 teaspoons olive oil

1 teaspoon balsamic vinegar

¼ cup (½ oz/15 g) torn basil leaves

2 slices prosciutto

2 eggs

2 bread rolls

2 slices cheese

freshly ground pepper

¼ cup (1 oz/30 g) shaved parmesan

Cook asparagus in simmering water for 1 to 2 minutes. Drain and refresh under cold water.

Heat butter in saucepan over medium heat until golden. Add oil, vinegar and basil and set aside.

Broil (grill) prosciutto until crisp.

Poach eggs in simmering water for 2 minutes.

Halve bread rolls and top with cheese slices. Sprinkle with pepper and broil (grill) until cheese is melted. Close rolls.

Divide asparagus between two plates, top with eggs and pour dressing over. Top with prosciutto and shaved parmesan and serve with warm cheese rolls.

Tip

It really doesn't matter what cheese you use for the warm cheese rolls—Emmental, Swiss, cheddar, whatever you have in the refrigerator.

Baked potatoes with fillings

Preparation: 2 minutes

Cooking time: 65minutes

Serves: 4

4 very large oval waxy potatoes, scrubbed but not peeled

choice of filling, about 2–3 tablespoons each (see Filling suggestions)

Preheat oven to 400°F (200°C/Gas 4).

Place potatoes directly on the oven rack and bake for 1 hour. Insert a skewer into the middle. If it slides in easily and comes out coated in potato, they are ready. Remove and let cool—until you can handle them.

While potatoes are cooking, prepare filling.

Cut potatoes in half lengthwise and scoop out the center, leaving about ¼ inch (0.5 cm) to form a shell inside. Mix potato flesh in a bowl with choice of filling.

Scoop potato back into skin casing and top with any garnish. Place on baking sheet and return to oven 5–10 minutes to warm through.

Filling suggestions

- Drained canned tuna with aioli

- Drained canned tuna mixed with a dash of sesame oil, dash of vinegar, a spoonful of grated ginger and some sesame seeds

- Pesto with parmesan and ricotta

- Chopped fresh dill, diced hard-cooked (boiled) eggs and cottage cheese

- Chopped salami, fried with diced tomato and green bell pepper (capsicum)

- Sautéed onion, prepared mustard, and Worcestershire sauce

- Sautéed sliced leek and bacon pieces

- Sautéed onion and tomato with basil

- Diced ham, cubes of cheddar or mozzarella, and dried or fresh oregano

- Crushed garlic, grated gruyere, dash of milk or cream and cracked pepper

- Chili beans, topped with sour cream, grated cheese, and with guacamole to serve

Baked vegetables Mediterranean-style

Preparation: 10 minutes

Cooking time: 30–60 minutes

Serves: 4

1 large, or 8 baby eggplants (aubergines)

4 zucchini (courgettes), halved lengthwise

salt

2 red bell peppers (capsicum), halved and seeded

2 leeks, halved lengthwise

2 plum (egg) tomatoes, halved, or ½ punnet of
  cherry tomatoes

1 cup (5 oz/150 g) black olives

½ cup (4 fl oz/125 ml) extra virgin olive oil

4 cloves garlic, chopped

salt and freshly ground black pepper

crusty white bread, to serve

Preheat oven to 475°F (240°C/Gas 9).

If using large eggplant, cut into slices about ½ inch
(1 cm) thick, or cut baby eggplants in half lengthwise.
Sprinkle this and zucchini with salt and let stand for
10 minutes or longer for juices to disgorge, then pat dry
with paper towel. Meanwhile, prepare other vegetables.

Place vegetables in large baking dish and drizzle with
olive oil (you may like to brush to ensure they are well-
coated). Sprinkle with garlic, salt and pepper.

Bake on highest shelf for about 30 to 60 minutes,
regularly basting or brushing with olive oil. The
vegetables will soften and caramelize, turning dark
brown on the edges. If vegetables are cooking unevenly,
remove cooked ones from oven and return near the end
to warm through.

If desired, warm bread in the oven on a separate shelf in
the last few minutes.

Tips

- Other vegetables that work well include: halved bulbs
  of fennel, whole baby squash, peeled onions (either
  whole or quartered), large flat mushroom caps. Smaller
  vegetable pieces may need to be added later in the
  cooking time.

- Sprinkle with fresh rosemary or chopped basil or dried
  oregano leaves before roasting. For more Middle
  Eastern flavors, try ground cumin and cayenne pepper.

- Crumble 3 oz (90 g) goat cheese or feta on top when
  serving.

- Cut cooked vegetables into chunks and toss through
  pasta with goat cheese or parmesan shavings.

- Serve hot or cold with couscous.

- Toss hot (or at room temperature) through mixed salad
  greens and dress with 1 tablespoon balsamic or red
  wine vinegar.

Bread salad with tomato and mozarella

Preparation: 15 minutes
Serves: 2

¼ loaf Italian-style bread, quartered lengthwise and
   cut into ¼-inch (1-cm) pieces
2 plum (egg) tomatoes, chopped
3½ oz (100 g) mozzarella, sliced
½ small purple onion, thinly sliced
1 teaspoon drained capers
¼ cup (½ oz/15 g) basil leaves
4 slices prosciutto (optional)
1 cooked chicken breast, chopped (optional)
small olives, to serve (optional)
grated parmesan, to serve (optional)
2 teaspoons balsamic vinegar
2 tablespoons olive oil
½ teaspoon Dijon mustard
1 small clove garlic, minced
salt and freshly ground pepper

Combine all salad ingredients in bowl.

Whisk together balsamic vinegar, oil, mustard, garlic and
salt and pepper. Pour over salad and let stand 5 minutes
before serving.

Tips

- Regular fresh mozzarella can be used for this recipe, or
  try bocconcini (the small white balls of fresh mozzarella
  that are also known as buffalo mozzarella in some
  countries).

- You can leave out the chicken and serve the salad as a
  side dish to any broiled (grilled) or panfried meat.

- Microwaved leeks make a simple but delicious
  accompaniment. Wash 1 small leek and cut into ¼-inch
  (1-cm) pieces. Place in covered microwave dish and
  microwave on high until tender, for 4 to 5 minutes.
  Season to taste with salt and freshly ground pepper,
  then stir through 2 teaspoons olive oil and serve warm.

Cabbage dolmas

Preparation: 20 minutes

Cooking time: 20 minutes

Serves: 4

4 oz (100 g) cooked rice

2–3 scallions (shallots/spring onions) trimmed and
   chopped

2 oz (50 g) chopped hazelnuts

½ small red bell pepper (capsicum), seeded and
   finely chopped

2 oz (60 g) mushrooms, finely chopped

salt and pepper

½ level teaspoon dried mixed herbs

¼ level teaspoon ground coriander

1 egg, beaten

1 cup (8 fl oz/250 ml) stock (vegetable or chicken)

approx. ¾ cup (5 fl oz/150 ml) milk or skimmed milk

2 level teaspoons cornstarch (cornflour)

8–12 large green cabbage leaves

Put rice into a bowl and mix in the scallions, hazelnuts,
bell pepper and mushrooms. Add seasonings, herbs and
coriander, mix well and bind with the egg.

Trim the tough base stem from each cabbage leaf and
blanch leaves in boiling water for 2 minutes. Drain well.
Put a spoonful of the stuffing at the stem end of each
leaf, fold in the edges and roll up to completely enclose
the filling. Place in a pan in a single layer.

Pour the stock onto the dolmas, bring to a boil, and
simmer gently for 15 minutes.

Transfer the dolmas to a serving dish and keep warm.

Make the cooking juices up to 1¼ cups (10 fl oz/300 ml)
with the milk, return to the pan and thicken with the
cornstarch blended in a little of the milk. Bring back to a
boil until thickened, season to taste, and pour over the
dolmas.

Tip

Dolmas can also be cooked in the microwave: on
maximum (100%) for 5 to 7 minutes.

Carrot nutburgers

Preparation: 20 minutes

Cooking time: 30 minutes

Serves: 4

1 onion, peeled and chopped

1 clove garlic, crushed

2 tablespoons butter or margarine

¼ cup (1 oz/30 g) all-purpose (plain) flour

½ cup (4 fl oz/125 ml) vegetable stock

2 cups (8 oz/250 g) mixed chopped nuts

2 oz (50 g) fresh breadcrumbs, brown or white

2 carrots, peeled and coarsely grated

1 level tablespoon freshly chopped parsley

1 level tablespoon dried thyme

1 tablespoon lemon juice

salt and pepper

1 level teaspoon vegetable extract

Preheat oven to 350°F (180°C/Gas 4).

Fry the onion and garlic in the butter until soft, but not colored. Stir in the flour and cook for a minute or two. Gradually add the stock and bring to the boil. Remove from the heat and stir in the nuts, breadcrumbs, carrots, parsley, thyme, lemon juice, seasonings and vegetable extract; let stand until cold.

Divide the mixture into four and shape into round burgers or cutlet shapes and place on a greased baking sheet. Cook in the oven for about 25 minutes, or until lightly browned and crisp.

Serve hot or cold, garnished with salad.

French omelette

Preparation: 1 minutes

Cooking time: 3–4 minutes

Serves: 1

2 eggs

1 tablespoon cold water

pinch of salt

freshly ground black pepper

2 teaspoons butter

Place eggs, water, salt and pepper to taste in a bowl and whisk lightly to combine.

Melt butter in a 7- to 8-inch (18- to 20-cm) omelette pan or small frying pan over medium-low heat, until butter is foaming. Tilt pan to coat bottom completely with butter.

Pour in egg mixture and cook, stirring once or twice, 1 minute. Cook without stirring, for 2 to 3 minutes more, or until eggs are cooked as desired—use a metal spatula or knife to lift edges occasionally, allowing uncooked mixture to flow underneath,

To serve, tilt pan away from you. Fold the upper third of omelette (closest to the handle) over the middle third, then tip pan and roll omelette onto a serving plate. Serve immediately.

Tips

• Avoid cooking omelette over too high heat or for too long—it will become tough and dry. Eggs should be just set but still moist on the top and firm and golden on the bottom.

• Use 1 to 2 tablespoons of any of the following, spooned over as omelette cooks, folded in as a filling, or as a topping or side dish: crumbled cooked bacon, sautéed sliced mushrooms, grated cheese, chopped scallions (spring onions/shallots), chopped fresh herbs e.g. basil, parsley, cilantro (coriander), chives, dill or mint, or chopped tomato sautéed with garlic and basil.

Gado gado

Preparation: 2 minutes
Cooking time: 15 minutes
Serves: 4

2 tablespoons peanut oil
1 onion, finely chopped
1 large clove garlic, crushed
1 teaspoon ginger, crushed
6 tablespoons peanut butter
1/3 cup (3 fl oz/90 ml) coconut milk or chicken stock
1/2 teaspoon blachan (shrimp paste) (optional)
1 tablespoon soy sauce, or to taste
2 teaspoons palm sugar or brown sugar
1/4 teaspoon minced chili (sambal olek), or to taste
1 teaspoon lemon juice
slices of prepared cold vegetables: try a mixture of
    shredded lettuce or cabbage, julienned cucumber
    and carrots, chopped tomato, boiled potato, hard-
    cooked (boiled) eggs, blanched snow peas (mange
    tout) and broccoli

Place oil, onion, garlic and ginger in small saucepan over medium heat and fry until onion is soft. Blend in peanut butter and coconut milk. Mix in blachan, soy sauce, sugar, chili and lemon juice and simmer over low heat for 5 to 10 minutes to develop.

Arrange vegetables on a patter and pour sauce over. Serve sauce warm or at room temperature.

Tips

- Use coconut milk rather than stock if you want a richer, creamier sauce.

- For a runnier sauce, dilute with hot water.

- If you can't use shrimp paste, try adding fish sauce (nam pla) to taste.

- For extra nuttiness, add a couple of tablespoons of crushed peanuts with onions.

- This peanut sauce also works well on chicken, beef or pork satés. Cut meat into 1-inch (2-cm) cubes, thread onto bamboo skewers that have been soaked in water, and broil (grill) or barbecue until cooked through. You can prepare them in advance and marinate the meat for several hours or overnight in a mixture of peanut or olive oil, chopped garlic and ginger.

Garlic mushrooms

Preparation: 15 minutes
Cooking time: 10 minutes
Serves: 4

1 lb (500 g) closed-cup mushrooms or button
  mushrooms
³/₄ cup (3 oz/90 g) butter or margarine
3–4 cloves garlic, crushed
1 tablespoon lemon juice
salt and freshly ground black pepper
1–2 level tablespoons freshly chopped mixed herbs or
  chopped parsley and chives
4 slices toast, to serve

Trim and wipe the mushrooms and, if large, cut into halves
or quarters. Buttons can be left whole if small.

Melt the butter in a pan and add the garlic. Cook for about
a minute then add the mushrooms and cook for 3 to
5 minutes, shaking and stirring almost all the time until
they are just lightly cooked.

Remove from the heat, add the lemon juice and
seasonings and then toss in most of the chopped herbs.
Return to the heat for about a minute to reheat. Serve
alone on a small plate or on pieces of toast and sprinkled
with the remaining herbs.

Tips
• Stir 3 to 4 tablespoons cream, sour cream or natural
  yogurt through the mushrooms just before serving. Toss
  with freshly cooked pasta.

• Can also be served with boiled long-grain rice.

Green vegetable pie

Preparation: 30 minutes (including thawing)
Cooking time: 30 minutes
Serves: 4

1 bunch silverbeet (Swiss chard)
10 oz (300 g) broccoli, cut into florets
2 zucchini (courgettes), thinly sliced
2 eggs, lightly beaten
3 tablespoons clear honey
6 sheets phyllo pastry, thawed
3 tablespoons butter, melted
2 cups grated cheddar

Preheat oven to 350°F (180°C/Gas 4).

Roughly tear the silverbeet and wash and drain well.

Place all vegetables, eggs, and honey in a large bowl and toss well to combine. Pack mixture tightly into shallow baking dish (about 10 x 8 inch/25 x 20 cm). Cover with 2 sheets of pastry, tucking in the sides, and brush with butter. Continue to layer pastry on top, two sheets at a time, brushing each layer with butter.

Bake for 30 minutes or until pastry is golden brown. Let rest a few minutes. Serve hot or cold.

Tip
If you keep your honey in the refrigerator, heat it in a microwave for 10 to 20 seconds to make it runny.

Leek and zucchini gratin

Preparation: 20 minutes

Cooking time: 5 minutes

Serves: 4

3 leeks (approx. 1 lb/500 g), trimmed

salt and pepper

3 zucchini (courgettes) (³/₄–1 lb/375–500 g) trimmed

2–3 tablespoons (1–1¹/₂ oz/30–45 g) butter or
  margarine

4 tablespoons light (single) cream or plain (natural)
  yogurt

2 level tablespoons fresh breadcrumbs

2 level tablespoons grated parmesan

2 level tablespoons very finely chopped red bell
  pepper (capsicum), blanched, to serve

Cut the leeks into quarters lengthwise then into lengths of approx. 2¹/₂ inches (6 cm). Blanch in boiling salted water for 2 to 3 minutes. Drain thoroughly and keep warm.

Cut the zucchini into narrow strips or thin slices and blanch for 1¹/₂ to 2 minutes and drain thoroughly.

Melt the butter in a nonstick pan and toss in first the leeks and then the zucchini. Heat for 2 to 3 minutes, shaking the pan frequently and stirring carefully to prevent them breaking up. Season well.

Turn into flameproof dish, spoon the cream over and then sprinkle with a mixture of crumbs and grated cheese. Place under a fairly low broiler (griller) for a few minutes until lightly browned.

Serve sprinkled with finely chopped bell pepper.

Onion and cheese flan

Preparation: 2–5 minutes

Cooking time: 30 minutes

Serves: 4

2 tablespoons butter

¼ cup (2 fl oz/60 ml) water

½ teaspoon salt

1½ cups (5½ oz/165 g) onions, thinly sliced

1 sheet frozen shortcrust pastry, thawed

3 eggs, lightly beaten

½ cup (4 fl oz/125 ml) milk

⅓ cup cheese, grated

Preheat oven to 375°F (190°C/Gas 5).

Melt butter with water and salt in saucepan. Add onions, cover tightly, and cook over low heat until onion is soft. Drain.

Meanwhile, line a lightly greased pan with pastry.

Combine eggs, milk, and cheese. Add onions, mix well, and pour into pastry case. Bake for about 25 minutes, or until a knife inserted in the middle comes out clean. Let stand for 5 minutes if serving hot. Can also be served cold.

Tips

- You can make individual flans using small pans.

- A shallow, rectangular baking dish will work instead of a quiche dish or pie pan; adjust quantity to suit.

- If you need more than a single sheet of pastry to cover the base of your pan, brush the edge of one with water, overlap it by about ½ inch (1 cm) with the other sheet and press down firmly to join.

- Use cream or half milk/half cream for a richer filling. Or just the yolk of the third egg.

- The cheese you use will affect the taste. Swiss or gruyere work well.

- Use leeks instead of onions in exactly the same way. Add some bacon at the same time if desired.

- Lay slices of tomato, black olives, and anchovy fillets on top of the filling before baking (pictured). Spinach works well with this combination—steam it first.

- Add a few tablespoons of grated parmesan and a few chopped basil leaves to the egg mixture. Lay tomato slices on top and additional slices of gruyere.

- Chopped fresh herbs always work—try oregano or thyme.

Oriental noodles with vegetables

Preparation: 15 minutes

Cooking time: 6–8 minutes

Serves: 4

1 tablespoon chopped fresh cilantro (coriander) leaves

2 tablespoons peanut oil

2 tablespoons lime or lemon juice

1 tablespoon sweet chili sauce

1 tablespoon soy sauce, preferably light

10 oz (300 g) fine Chinese egg noodles

2 tablespoons peanut oil

4 oz (125 g) snow peas (mange tout)

1 red bell pepper (capsicum)

4 oz (125 g) oyster or button mushrooms

4 scallions (spring onions/shallots) with some green tops

1 clove garlic

1 tablespoon peeled, grated fresh ginger

1 tablespoon sesame seeds

Place cilantro, oil, lemon juice, chili and soy sauce in a screw-top jar, cover and shake well to blend.

Soak noodles in a bowl of hot water for 10 minutes or until strands separate; drain. Cook noodles in a large saucepan of boiling water for 2 to 3 minutes or until al dente. Drain and rinse under cold running water. Drain again and toss with 1 tablespoon peanut oil.

Meanwhile, trim stem ends from snow peas. Halve bell pepper, remove seeds and cut into thin strips. Thinly slice mushrooms and scallions. Peel and slice garlic.

Heat remaining peanut oil in a wok or large, heavy-based frying pan over high heat. Add garlic and ginger and stir-fry for 1 minute. Add snow peas and bell pepper and stir-fry for 2 to 3 minutes or until snow peas turn bright green. Add mushrooms, scallions, noodles and dressing and heat through, stirring.

Spread sesame seeds on baking sheet and toast under hot broiler (grill). Sprinkle onto noodles and serve immediately.

Tips

• Chinese egg noodles can be purchased in bundles in both fine and thicker widths from oriental food stores and supermarkets. If using wide noodles, cook them for 3 to 5 minutes.

• Try adding 8 to 12 oz (250 to 375 g) flaked poached fish or finely sliced cooked chicken.

Pizzas à la gourmet

Preparation: 5–10 minutes
Cooking time: 5–20 minutes
Serves: 2

pre-prepared pizza base
enough tomato paste to cover base
dried oregano, as desired
cheese, grated, as desired
vegetables, as desired
fresh basil, to serve

Preheat oven according to pizza base instructions.

Spread tomato paste over base and sprinkle with oregano. Top with cheese and vegetables of choice.

Cook in oven for about 10 to 20 minutes.

Top with fresh basil before serving.

Tips

- Make pizzas small sizes to feed one or two, in larger sizes for more, or make an assortment to feed a crowd.

- For the base, you can also use pita bread (brushed with oil), flour tortilla (brushed with oil and pricked with a fork), foccacia bread, Turkish pidé bread, split open, or squares of frozen puff pastry (thawed, brushed with melted butter, and cooked in a moderate oven after topping according to time on packet).

- Depending on the base, you cook pizza by placing under broiler (grill) for a few minutes until the top has heated and the cheese has melted.

- Other toppings could include:

   — spread the base with Mexican tomato salsa. Add shredded chicken and slices of avocado, and top with cheddar or Monterey jack cheese;

   — spread the base with tomato paste and sprinkle with fresh or dried thyme. Add slices of purple onion, black olives and fillets of sardines (from the can and drained);

   — spread the base with pesto. Add shaved ham, toasted pine nuts and sun-dried tomatoes and bell peppers (capsicums), and top with grated parmesan;

   — spread the base with hummus. Add slices of roasted eggplant (aubergine) and top with crumbled goat cheese;

   — spread the base with tapenade. Cover with caramelized onion (slow-cooked in a frying pan with butter until ultra-soft). Top with slices of tomato and parmesan shavings, or small pieces of boiled sweet potato.

Potato and pea curry

Preparation: 5 minutes

Cooking time: 25 minutes

Serves: 4

1½ lb (750 g) potatoes, peeled and cut into large
  chunks

2 tablespoons vegetable oil

2 cloves garlic, finely chopped

1 medium onion, finely chopped

2 teaspoon ginger, grated

2 teaspoons hot chili (such as sambel olek), minced

¼ teaspoon cardamom seeds—cracked

½ teaspoon cumin

1 teaspoon turmeric

½ teaspoon garam masala

1 teaspoon salt

pepper, to taste

¼ teaspoon ground cinnamon

3 cloves

1 bay leaf

1 tablespoon lemon juice

2 cups rice, to serve

1 cup frozen peas

4 tablespoons water

Parboil potatoes in salted water for 10 minutes. Drain
and set aside.

Heat oil in a large saucepan. Add garlic and onion and
sauté until onion is soft. Add spices and lemon juice and
fry gently for a few minutes.

Put rice on to cook.

Add potatoes, peas, and water to onion mixture and mix
well to combine. Cover tightly and cook 10 minutes.

Serve hot with steamed rice.

Tips

- Of course, like all curries, it tastes even better the next
  day.

- Add 1 teaspoon mustard seeds after cooking onion,
  and fry until they start to pop.

- Use less potato and instead add 5 oz (150 g)
  pumpkin, peeled and cut into large chunks. Add to
  boiling potatoes after 5 minutes.

- Before serving, sprinkle the curry with 4 tablespoons
  shredded coconut that has been lightly toasted under
  the broiler (griller).

Potato wedges with aioli

Preparation: 5 minutes

Cooking time: 40 minutes

Serves: 3–4

6 large waxy, white-fleshed potatoes, scrubbed clean

1 teaspoon salt

4 tablespoons all-purpose (plain) flour

1 teaspoon paprika

1/2 teaspoon cayenne pepper

2 tablespoons olive oil or melted butter

salt and freshly ground black pepper, to serve

2 cloves garlic, crushed

3/4 cup (6 fl oz/180 ml) whole-egg mayonnaise

pinch of salt

generous squeeze of lemon juice, to taste

salsa, to serve (optional)

Place potatoes in boiling salted water and cook until just tender but not too soft, about 15 to 20 minutes. Drain, peel and slice each potato into quarters lengthwise to form wedges. Pat dry with a cloth.

Preheat oven to 400°F (200°C/Gas 4).

Mix salt, flour, paprika and cayenne pepper in a large bowl. Toss wedges first in oil or butter to coat, then in flour mixture. Bake in a baking dish for about 20 minutes, turning after 10 minutes, until crispy and golden brown.

Meanwhile, to make aioli, mix garlic into mayonnaise. Add salt and lemon juice.

Serve sprinkled with salt and pepper, and accompanied by aioli and salsa.

Quiche with saucepan pastry

Preparation: 10–15 minutes

Cooking time: 40–45 minutes

Serves: 6

⅔ cup (5 fl oz/150 ml) milk

4 oz (125 g) butter, cut into pieces

2 cups (8 oz/250 g) all-purpose (plain) flour

1½ teaspoons baking powder

pinch of salt

3–4 slices bacon

½ bunch scallions (shallots/spring onions), with
   some green tops

1½ cups (6 oz/180 g) grated cheddar or Swiss
cheese

3 eggs

¾ cup (6 fl oz/180 ml) milk

¾ cup (6 fl oz/180 ml) light (single) cream

1 tablespoon all-purpose (plain) flour

2 teaspoons Dijon mustard

freshly ground black pepper

To make pastry, warm milk and butter in a large
saucepan over medium heat until butter just melts.
Remove from heat and let cool slightly. Sift together flour,
baking powder and salt. Add, all at once, to milk
mixture. Beat with a wooden spoon until just blended
and smooth. Press warm mixture evenly into base and
sides of a 10-inch (25-cm) fluted pie (flan) ring with
removable base. Trim edges to rim of pan with a sharp
knife.

Preheat oven to 400°F (200°C/Gas 6).

To make filling, remove rind and discard; coarsely chop
bacon. Heat a small frying pan over medium heat. Add
bacon and sauté until just golden. Remove bacon with a
slotted spoon and scatter over pastry. Thinly slice
scallions. Scatter with cheese over bacon.

Whisk together eggs, milk, cream, flour, mustard and
black pepper. Carefully pour mixture over filling.

Bake for 10 minutes. Reduce oven temperature to 350°F
(180°C/Gas 4) and bake for 30 to 35 minutes or until
filling is set and pastry is crusty and golden. Let stand 5
to for 10 minutes in pan to let filling settle. Cut into
wedges to serve.

Tips

• Instead of scallions, you can use 10 oz (300 g) frozen
  chopped spinach which has been thawed and
  squeezed dry; a combination of cooked green peas
  and whole kernel corn; 1 to 1¼ cups (10 to 12 oz/
  300 to 375 ml) chopped cooked vegetables.

• Instead of bacon, use 6 to 8 oz (180 to 250 g) diced
  leg ham, thinly sliced cooked chicken or drained
  canned red salmon or chunk-style tuna.

Ratatouille

Preparation: 50 minutes

Cooking time: 25–30 minutes

Serves: 4

1 eggplant (aubergine)

salt

2 onions

2 cloves garlic

2 green or red bell peppers (capsicum) or a
   combination

2 zucchini (courgettes)

3 large ripe tomatoes

1/3 cup (3 fl oz/90 ml) olive oil

freshly ground black pepper

4 sprigs fresh parsley, leaves only, to serve (optional)

Cut eggplant crosswise into 1/4-inch (5-mm) slices then cut each slice into halves or quarters. Place in a colander, sprinkling layers liberally with salt, and stand in sink or over a bowl for 30 minutes to disgorge juices.

Meanwhile, peel onion and slice into rings. Peel and thinly slice garlic. Halve bell peppers, remove seeds and cut into thick strips. Cut zucchini crosswise into 1/2-inch (1-cm) thick rounds. Slice tomatoes.

Rinse eggplant under cold running water to remove salt. Drain and dry with paper towel.

Drizzle 1 tablespoon oil in a large, heavy-based saucepan, then arrange vegetable layers in pan in this order: onion, garlic, bell pepper, eggplant, zucchini, tomatoes. Sprinkle with black pepper to taste and drizzle with remaining oil.

Cover pan and cook over low to medium heat, without stirring, for 20 to 30 minutes or until vegetables are tender. Chop parsley and sprinkle over vegetables before serving.

Tips

- Serve with grilled or roasted meats and poultry, or as a meatless main course with pasta (pictured), rice or couscous. Serve cold as part of an antipasti tray or summer salad platter.

- A splash of red or white wine or lemon juice, a handful of marinated black olives and a sprinkling of chopped fresh or dried herbs (e.g. oregano or basil) can be added when layering vegetables.

- When ripe fresh tomatoes are not available, use a 14 oz (440 g) can of whole, peeled tomatoes. Crush tomatoes before adding. Uncover pan during last 5 to 10 minutes of cooking to allow excess moisture to evaporate.

Scrambled eggs

Preparation: 2–5 minutes

Cooking time: 5 minutes

Serves: 2–3

4 large (2 oz/60 g each) egg

4 tablespoons milk

salt and freshly ground black pepper, to taste

2 teaspoons butter

Place eggs and milk in a bowl with salt and pepper to taste. Whisk to combine.

Melt butter in a heavy-based saucepan over low heat. Add egg mixture and cook, occasionally stirring gently, until mixture is set but still creamy. Serve immediately.

Tips

• To microwave: melt butter in a small, microwavable dish. Add whisked eggs, milk and salt and pepper to dish. Cook on medium (50%), stirring once or twice, 1½ to 2 minutes or until set but still creamy.

• If eggs are cold from the refrigerator, rinse briefly under warm running water.

• Serving suggestions: for a gourmet brunch or supper dish, add one of the following combinations to scrambled eggs. Heat through and serve with toasted bagels or another interesting type of bread:

— bacon, parsley and cracked pepper;

— strips of smoked salmon, snipped fresh chives, freshly ground black pepper (pictured);

— grated gruyère or emmenthal cheese, sautéed mushrooms and steamed fresh asparagus spears;

— finely chopped sun-dried tomatoes, red and green bell peppers (capsicum), and scallions (shallots/spring onions) with grated mature cheddar and a dash of hot pepper sauce.

Sesame stir-fried green vegetables

Preparation: 10 minutes

Cooking time: 8–10 minutes

Serves: 4

1-inch (2.5-cm) piece fresh ginger

2 cloves garlic

6 scallions (spring onions/shallots)

2 sticks celery

8–10 asparagus spears, green beans or snow peas
   (mange tout), or a combination

2 medium unpeeled zucchini (courgettes)

8 oyster mushrooms, optional

6 oz (180 g) English spinach or young silverbeet
   (Swiss chard) leaves

1 tablespoon sesame seeds

2 tablespoons vegetable or peanut oil

½ teaspoon sesame oil

1 tablespoon dry sherry

1 tablespoon soy sauce, preferably light

Prepare vegetables. With a small vegetable knife, peel ginger, slice thinly then cut into slivers. Peel garlic and slice thinly. Trim coarse green tops from scallions, leaving about 1 inch (2.5 cm) of tender green attached. Cut lengthwise in half. Cut celery into long diagonal slices. Trim tough ends from asparagus, and stalk ends from green beans or snow peas. Cut into 2- to 3 -inch (5- to 7.5-cm) lengths or leave whole. Cut zucchini into sticks of the same size. Leave mushrooms whole. Rinse spinach and remove any coarse stems.

Toast sesame seeds by placing in a small nonstick frying pan over medium heat. Stir frequently until golden. Remove immediately from pan (to prevent overbrowning) and let cool.

Place a wok or deep, heavy-based frying pan with sloping sides over high heat. When hot, add oils and swirl pan to coat sides. Add ginger, garlic and scallions to pan and stir-fry 30 seconds. Add celery, asparagus and zucchini. Stir-fry for 3 to 5 minutes or until bright green and almost tender. Add mushrooms, spinach, sherry and soy sauce and stir-fry until leaves are wilted and vegetables are cooked to your liking (they should be tender but still crisp).

Sprinkle with sesame seeds and serve immediately.

Tips

- Serve with brown rice, Chinese noodles or couscous.

- For even cooking, cut vegetables into same-size pieces.

- For authenticity, substitute sake or mirin (the latter is sweeter) for sherry. Both these rice wines are available at specialist food stores and major supermarkets.

Spanish tortilla

Preparation: 10 minutes

Cooking time: 30minutes

Serves: 4

4 medium potatoes (about 14 oz/400 g)

¼ cup (2 fl oz/60 ml) olive oil

1 onion, chopped

½ red bell pepper (capsicum), chopped

4 eggs

½ teaspoon salt

freshly ground black pepper

6 anchovy fillets, drained

Peel and dice potatoes into ½-inch (1-cm) cubes. Pat dry with paper towel.

Heat oil in in a heavy-based frying pan until smoking. Add potatoes in a single layer and cook slowly over medium heat for about 15 minutes, stirring occasionally—they should become only lightly golden (do not allow them to crisp). When tender, remove from pan and fry onion and pepper in pan until tender, about 3 minutes.

Beat eggs with salt and pepper. Combine in a bowl with potatoes, onion and pepper.

There should be about 1 tablespoon of oil left in the frying pan. If not, add some more. Heat until smoking, then pour in egg and potato mixture. Lay anchovies fillets on top. Cook on low heat until most of the egg has set, about 5 minutes. To cook egg on top, pop pan under broiler (grill), leaving the handle to stick out if it isn't heatproof.

Tips

- For a classic tortilla española, leave out the red pepper and anchovies—purists don't even use the onion. If you can be bothered, slice the potatoes very thinly instead of dicing them. Cook in batches, a single layer at a time, without letting them crisp. The extra effort pays off with improved taste and texture.

- You can add almost anything your heart desires: diced chorizo or ham can be fried with the onions. Or you could add some green in the form of peas or shredded arugula (rocket). Freshly chopped parsley or basil can be added to the eggs, as can grated cheese.

- The potatoes can also be cooked in stock. Fry them for a few minutes in a couple of tablespoons of olive oil over medium-high heat, until golden. Then add a cup of stock and simmer potatoes until tender.

Spicy egg Mexican tortillas

Preparation: 10 minutes

Cooking time: 20 minutes

Serves: 4

2 tablespoons vegetable oil

1 medium onion, finely chopped

2 cloves garlic, minced

2 teaspoons ground cumin

2 large tomatoes, chopped

2 jalapeño chilies, finely chopped

2 medium-size red bell peppers (capsicums),
   roasted, peeled and chopped

1 tablespoon butter

10 eggs, lightly beaten

3 tablespoons chopped fresh cilantro (coriander)
   leaves

4 large corn or flour tortillas

1 tablespoon water

3 oz (90 g) cheddar, grated

2 scallions (shallots/spring onions), chopped

Preheat oven to 400°F (200°C/Gas 6). Heat oil in large frying pan over medium heat. Add onion and garlic and cook, stirring, until onion is soft. Add cumin, tomatoes, chilies and bell peppers and cook, stirring, until liquid is evaporated, about 5 minutes.

Heat butter in another pan over low heat. Add eggs and stir gently until just set. Spoon eggs and coriander into tomato mixture; stir gently to combine and reheat.

Meanwhile, lightly sprinkle tortillas with water. Wrap in aluminum foil and heat in oven for 5 minutes. Sprinkle egg mixture with cheese and scallions and roll in warmed tortillas.

Tips

- If jalapeños not available, a small hot red chili will suffice.

- You can use any cheese you like in this recipe.

Spicy peanut noodles

Preparation: 5 minutes

Cooking time: 10 minutes

Serves: 4

1 lb (500 g) Chinese noodles

1 tablespoon peanut oil

1 lb (500 g) chicken fillet, cut into strips

1 tablespoon crunchy peanut butter

juice of 1/2 lime (optional)

2 tablespoons sesame oil

1/4 cup (2 fl oz/60 ml) fish sauce (nam pla)

2 tablespoons soy sauce

1/2 teaspoon brown sugar

2 cloves garlic, minced

5 scallions (spring onions/shallots), chopped

1/3 cup peanuts, chopped fresh cilantro (coriander)
   leaves, to serve

Cook noodles in boiling water according to packet
instructions. Drain.

Meanwhile, heat oil in a wok or large pan and sauté
chicken strips.

Combine remaining ingredients in a small bowl. Add to
chicken with cooked noodles and toss through.

Serve warm, topped with peanuts and cilantro.

Tips

• Sauté 8 oz (250 g) raw shrimp (prawns) instead of the
  chicken. Or use cooked shrimp and toss with drained
  noodles.

• Add 7 oz (220 g) fresh or canned bean sprouts for extra
  crunch.

• Add 1 tablespoon blachan (shrimp paste) instead of fish
  sauce, and chili flakes as desired, for a really authentic
  taste.

• This dish can also be served chilled, as a salad.

Spinach and cheese phyllo parcels

Preparation: 20 minutes

Cooking: 20 minutes

Serves: 4

12 oz (375 g) fresh silverbeet (Swiss chard)

salt and pepper

4 oz (125 g) cottage cheese

3 oz (90 g) mature cheddar, grated

1 egg, beaten

small amount powdered garlic

good dash or Worcestershire sauce

1/4 level teaspoon ground coriander

8 sheets phyllo pastry

2 tablespoons butter, melted

Preheat oven to 400°F (200°C/Gas Mark 6).

Trim the silverbeet, wash thoroughly and put into a pan. Add a little boiling water and a pinch of salt and cook until very tender.

Beat the cottage cheese, cheddar, egg, garlic, Worcestershire sauce and coriander together in a bowl.

Drain the Swiss chard thoroughly, using a potato masher to remove all the water. Cool a little then chop finely and beat into the cheese mixture.

Spread out the sheets of pastry and brush each lightly with melted butter.

Divide the filling into eight and spread one portion over about 1/8 of each piece of pastry, at one end, leaving a pastry margin each side. Fold over the margins to cover the edge of the filling and then fold up to make a parcel. Stand the parcels on a greased baking sheet and brush with the remaining butter.

Cook in the oven for about 20 minutes, or until lightly gold, brown and crisp. Serve hot or cold.

Spinach tart

Preparation: 10 minutes

Cooking time: 15–35 minutes

Serves: 2–3

2 teaspoons olive oil

4 scallions (shallots/spring onions), chopped

1 slice bacon, chopped

1 clove garlic, minced

2 cups (9 oz/270 g) cooked, drained English spinach

½ cup (1 oz/30 g) chopped fresh basil

5 oz (150 g) fresh ricotta

3 oz (90 g) feta, crumbled

2 tablespoons grated parmesan

2 eggs

1 cup (8 fl oz/250 ml) milk

salt and freshly ground pepper

Heat oil in frying pan over medium heat. Add scallions, bacon and garlic and cook for 5 minutes.

Heat oven to 350°F (180°C/Gas 4) if you will be baking the tart (it can also be microwaved).

Transfer bacon mixture to bowl and stir in spinach, basil and cheeses. Place in microwave-proof or ovenproof pie dish. Combine eggs and milk and pour over. Season with salt and pepper.

Bake for 30 minutes or microwave on high until set, 10 to 15 minutes.

Serve warm, cut into wedges.

Stuffed red peppers

Preparation: 10 minutes

Cooking time: 45 minutes

Serves: 4

1 tablespoon olive oil

1 medium onion, chopped

1 clove garlic, minced

5 oz (150 g) eggplant (aubergine), chopped

2 tablespoons chopped fresh parsley

½ oz (15 g) drained capers, chopped

6 anchovy fillets, chopped

2 large tomatoes, chopped

1 oz (30 g) parmesan, grated

½ cup (4 oz/125 g) cooked brown rice

2 large red bell peppers (capsicums)

2 tablespoons sour cream, to serve

Preheat oven to 350°F (180°C/Gas 4).

Heat oil in large frying pan over medium heat. Add onion and garlic and cook, stirring, until onion is soft. Stir in eggplant, parsley, capers, anchovies and tomatoes and cook, stirring, for 3 minutes. Stir in parmesan and rice. Remove from heat and let cool.

Cut bell peppers in half lengthwise, removing seeds and membranes. Place on baking sheet and fill with eggplant mixture. Bake until bell peppers are tender, about 40 minutes. Serve with small dollop of sour cream.

Tomato and feta cheese slices

Preparation: 5 minutes

Cooking time: 20 minutes

Serves: 4

1 sheet ready-rolled puff pastry, thawed

2 tablespoons olive oil

1 lb (500 g) cherry tomatoes

1 teaspoon sugar

5 oz (150 g) feta cheese, crumbled

3 tablespoons shredded fresh basil leaves, to serve

1 oz (30 g) shaved parmesan, to serve

Preheat oven to 400°F (200°C/Gas 6).

Place pastry on greased baking sheet and fold in edges to make a ³/₄-inch (2-cm) border; pinch corners together.

Heat oil in frying pan over medium heat. Add tomatoes and sugar and cook, stirring, until tomatoes are shiny, about 2 minutes.

Combine feta cheese and 2 tablespoons basil and spread over pastry base. Top with tomatoes. Bake until pastry is puffed and browned, about 15 minutes. Before serving, sprinkle with remaining basil and parmesan.

Tortilla chips with guacamole

Preparation: 15 minutes

Serves: 2

12 oz (375 g) corn tortilla chips, warmed

1 ripe avocado

2 teaspoons lime or lemon juice

1 tablespoon finely diced onion

1/4 teaspoon ground cumin

1 small red chili, finely chopped

2 tablespoons finely chopped fresh cilantro
   (coriander) leaves

1 small tomato, chopped

1/2 barbecued chicken, skin removed, shredded
   (optional)

1/4 large lettuce, finely shredded

1 large tomato, chopped

3 oz (90 g) fresh Mexican cheese, crumbled
   prepared salsa, store-bought or homemade

Preheat oven to 300°F (150°C/Gas 4).

Place tortilla chips on baking sheet and warm in oven,
about 10 minutes.

For guacamole, mash avocado and stir in lime juice,
onion, cumin, chili, cilantro and tomato.

Serve warmed chips piled with guacamole, shredded
chicken, lettuce, tomato, cheese and salsa.

Tips

• Instead of tortilla chips, use 4 to 6 warmed taco shells
  or corn or flour tortillas. Warm tortillas according to
  package directions—usually by turning with tongs in a
  hot ungreased frying pan for 30 seconds on each side.

• Feta cheese can be used in place of Mexican cheese.

• Note that guacamole cannot be made in advance, as
  avocado turns brown quickly.

Vegetable curry

Preparation: 10 minutes

Cooking time: 25–30 minutes

Serves: 4–6

8 oz (250 g) cauliflower

8 oz (250 g) broccoli

2 carrots or young parsnips

3–4 finger-thick eggplant (aubergines) or unpeeled
zucchini (courgettes)

4 oz (125 g) button mushrooms

6 oz (180 g) green beans or ½ cup (2 oz/60 g)
shelled fresh or frozen peas

1 large onion

2 cloves garlic

½-inch (1-cm) piece green ginger

2 tablespoons vegetable oil

1 tablespoon curry paste

1 teaspoon chopped fresh red chilies

14 oz (440 g) can whole peeled tomatoes

1½ cups (12 fl oz/375 ml) water or vegetable stock

2–3 tablespoons chopped fresh cilantro (coriander)
leaves, to serve (optional)

Prepare vegetables: cut cauliflower and broccoli into
florets. Peel and thickly slice carrots. Trim ends from
eggplant then halve or quarter lengthwise; salt eggplant
to degorge juices. Halve or quarter mushrooms. Trim
beans and cut into 2- to 3-inch (5- to 7.5-cm) lengths.

Peel onion and garlic and finely chop. Use a sharp knife
to peel ginger; thinly slice then cut into thin strips.

Heat oil in a large, heavy-based saucepan over medium
heat. Add onion, garlic, ginger, curry paste and chili and
cook, stirring, for 5 minutes or until onion is soft. Add
vegetables and cook, stirring, for 5 minutes. Add
undrained, crushed tomatoes and water to pan and
bring to boil. Reduce heat and simmer gently, stirring
occasionally, for 15 minutes, or until vegetables are
tender but still crisp.

Sprinkle with cilantro and serve.

Tips

- There are a number of commercially prepared curry
  pastes available from international sections in major
  supermarkets and oriental food stores. Experiment
  with them as they vary in flavor and intensity.

- Other suitable vegetables include: peeled and cubed
  yams (red sweet potatoes) or pumpkin; thickly sliced
  leek; fresh or frozen broad (fava) beans or lima beans;
  small squash.

- Use thick canned coconut milk instead of water or
  stock to make a slightly creamy, coconut version.

- Add ½ cup (4 oz/125 ml) rinsed and drained canned
  chickpeas (garbanzo beans), red kidney beans or
  cannellini beans and heat through just before serving.

desserts

Baked bananas

Preparation: 5 minutes

Cooking time: 15 minutes

Serves: 2

2 bananas, peeled and sliced

¼ cup (2½ oz/75 g) lightly packed brown sugar

2 tablespoons unsalted butter

1 tablespoon shredded coconut

2 tablespoons dark rum

ice cream, to serve

Preheat oven to 350°F (180°C/Gas 4).

Place bananas in small ovenproof dish. Sprinkle with sugar and dot with butter. Sprinkle with coconut.

Bake until bananas are soft and coconut is golden brown, 10 to 15 minutes. Pour rum over, gently stirring through. Serve bananas warm over ice cream.

Banana and raspberry soufflés

Preparation: 10 minutes

Cooking time: 15 minutes

Serves: 4

2 medium-size ripe bananas (10 oz/300 g)

1 tablespoon lemon juice

4 egg whites

¾ oz (25 g) powdered (icing) sugar

5 oz (150 g) raspberries

powdered (icing) sugar, to serve (optional)

Heat oven to 450°F (230°C/Gas 8). Lightly grease inside of four 1-cup (8 fl oz/250 ml) ramekins with butter or oil.

Mash bananas and lemon juice in bowl with fork until well combined, with no large lumps.

Beat egg whites in large bowl with electric mixer until soft peaks form. Gradually add sugar, beating until sugar is completely dissolved and stiff peaks form.

Gently fold egg whites into banana mixture, then gently fold in raspberries. Spoon mixture into prepared dishes and arrange on baking sheet. Bake for 15 minutes, or until puffed and browned.

Finish with light dusting of powdered sugar and serve immediately.

Tips

- Soufflés are not really as difficult as some people like to think. Simply have all the ingredients ready in advance so they can be put together quickly; and serve immediately.

- The raspberries can be replaced by whatever berry is in season, but any berry larger than your thumbnail is best cut in half.

Double chocolate and pistachio mousse

Preparation: 10 minutes plus 4 hours refrigeration
Cooking time: 10 minutes
Serves: 4

1¼ cups (10 fl oz/300 ml) light (single) cream
1 tablespoon unflavored gelatin
3 oz (90 g) semi-sweet (plain) chocolate, chopped
3 oz (90 g) milk chocolate, chopped
3 ice cubes
¾ cup (6 fl oz/180 ml) milk
¼ cup (2 oz/60 g) superfine (caster) sugar
¾ cup (3 oz/90 g) pistachio nuts, finely chopped

Pour half the cream into a small saucepan and sprinkle with gelatin. Let soften for 2 minutes. Place over medium heat and stir until gelatin dissolves completely. Remove from heat and stir in chocolate.

Blend or process mixture until chocolate has completely melted. Add ice, milk, sugar and remaining cream; blend or process until smooth.

Stir in half the pistachios. Divide mixture among four glasses, cover and refrigerate for 4 hours, or until set. Sprinkle with remaining nuts before serving.

Tips

• You can use any type of chocolate or nut, but blanched nuts are best.

• You can leave out nuts and add ¾ teaspoon of any flavoring extract you like, perhaps orange or peppermint.

• This dessert takes 4 hours to set, but it can be made two days in advance of serving.

Dried fruit compote with couscous and yogurt

Preparation: 10 minutes
Cooking time: 10–15 minutes
Serves: 4

8 oz (250 g) dried figs
8 oz (250 g) pitted (stoned) prunes
8 oz (250 g) dried apricots
4 oz (125 g) dried apples
2½ oz (75 g) sliced almonds
1 teaspoon cinnamon
2 tablespoons brown sugar
2 cups (16 fl oz/500 ml) orange juice
1¼ cups (8 oz/250 g) couscous
1 tablespoon butter
1 cup (8 fl oz/250 ml) plain (natural) yogurt
2 tablespoons honey
pinch of nutmeg
fresh mint leaves, to serve

Combine fruit, almonds, cinnamon, sugar and juice in medium saucepan over high heat and bring to a boil. Reduce heat to low, cover and simmer, stirring occasionally, until fruit is softened and fragrant, about 10 minutes.

Meanwhile, place couscous in heat-resistant bowl and pour in 1 cup (8 fl oz/250 ml) boiling water. Add butter and stir briefly to combine. Cover with plastic wrap for 3 minutes. Gently stir mixture with fork until grains are separated and lightly fluffed. Combine yogurt, honey and nutmeg in small bowl and mix well.

To serve, divide couscous among four deep bowls. Top with fruit mixture, pour some yogurt onto each serving and garnish with fresh mint leaves.

Tips

• Choose any fruit juice you like, or try ⅔ juice to ⅓ sweet wine.

• To save time and effort, you can use plain or pre-flavored yogurt and a packaged mixture of dried fruit.

Fresh berries in lemon syrup

Preparation and cooking time: 10 minutes
Serves: 2

¼ cup (2½ oz/75 g) superfine (caster) sugar

¼ cup (2 fl oz/60 ml) water

2 tablespoons lemon juice

1½ cups (about 8 oz/250 g) berries, such as
  raspberries, strawberries, blueberries and/or
  blackberries

thickened cream or heavy (double) cream or ice
  cream, to serve

Combine sugar, water and lemon juice in a small saucepan and stir over low heat to dissolve sugar. Bring to a boil, reduce heat and simmer for 2 minutes.

Remove syrup from heat and stir through berries. Let stand for 3 to 4 minutes so berries become slightly warm and soften.

Serve while still warm, with cream or ice cream.

Tips

• You can use mixed berries or just a single variety.

• You can substitute lime juice for lemon.

Jamaican banana cups

Preparation: 10 minutes

Cooking time: 20 minutes

Serves: 4

1 large orange

6 medium bananas (30 oz/90 g)

½ cup (3 oz/90 g) brown sugar, packed

6 tablespoons (3 oz/90 g) unsalted butter

6 tablespoons (3 fl oz/90 ml) dark rum

½ cup (1 oz/30 g) fresh breadcrumbs

3 tablespoons (1 oz/30 g) rolled oats

½ teaspoon ground cinnamon

6 tablespoons (3 fl oz/90 ml) heavy (double) cream, to serve

¾ cup (3 oz/90 g) chopped pecans, toasted, to serve

Heat oven to 400°F (200°C/Gas 6). Finely grate 1 teaspoon orange zest and squeeze 6 tablespoons (3 fl oz/90 ml) juice from the orange. Cut bananas into ¾-inch (2-cm) slices.

Combine ½ of the sugar, ⅓ of the butter and ½ of the rum in large frying pan. Cook over medium heat, stirring frequently, until sugar has dissolved and mixture is starting to bubble. Stir in bananas and toss until evenly coated. Remove from heat.

Divide half of banana mixture among four 1-cup (8 fl oz/ 250 ml) ramekins.

Sprinkle each with 1 tablespoon breadcrumbs. Top with remaining banana mixture. Spoon orange juice over each ramekin.

Combine remaining breadcrumbs, sugar and butter with oats, orange zest and cinnamon, blending with fingertips until mixture resembles coarse crumbs. Sprinkle over bananas.

Bake until topping is crisp and golden, about 15 minutes. Serve warm, topped with cream and sprinkled with nuts.

Tips

- To make fresh breadcrumbs, process fresh crustless white bread in a blender or food processor until fine crumbs form.

- When cooking rum mixture, be sure the heat is not too high or the rum will evaporate very quickly, or could even ignite—and this is not a flambé!

Lime and blueberry crème brûlée

Preparation: 10 minute plus 4 hours refrigeration
Cooking time: 25 minutes
Serves: 4

2 cups (16 fl oz/500 ml) heavy (double) cream
1 teaspoon vanilla
finely grated zest of 1 lime
5 egg yolks
scant ½ cup (3½ oz/100 g) superfine (caster) sugar
1 cup (4 oz/125 g) blueberries

Preheat oven to 400°F (200°C/Gas 6).

Bring cream to a boil in saucepan. Remove from heat and stir in vanilla and lime zest. Cover and allow flavors to infuse for 5 minutes.

Beat egg yolks with ¾ of the sugar, until slightly thickened. Slowly stir in hot cream mixture, blending well. Divide blueberries among four ¾-cup (6 fl oz/180 ml) ramekins and pour custard over.

Arrange ramekins in pan of hot water—hot water should reach at least halfway up sides of custard. Bake until a skin forms on surface of custard, 15 to 20 minutes. Let cool, then chill.

To serve, sprinkle each brûlée with remaining sugar and broil (grill) as close to heat as possible until sugar melts and caramelizes, about 2 minutes. Serve immediately.

Tips

• For best results, brûlées should be refrigerated for at least 4 hours after cooling, but they will last in the refrigerator for up to 4 days, so they can be made in advance.

• For a superb finish, invest in a hand-held gas blowtorch—this is an excellent tool for caramelizing all sorts of dishes.

Poached peaches with ricotta cream

Preparation and cooking time: 25 minutes
Serves: 2

2 cups (16 fl oz/500 ml) water
¾ cup (6 oz/180 g) sugar
2 medium-size ripe peaches (about 10 oz/300 g)
½ cup (4 oz/125 g) fresh ricotta
2 tablespoons heavy (double) cream
1 tablespoon lightly packed brown sugar

Combine water and sugar in saucepan and stir over low heat to dissolve sugar. Bring to a boil and reduce heat to a steady simmer. Add peaches and simmer for 15 minutes. Remove peaches with slotted spoon and set aside.

Bring syrup back to a boil and boil until reduced by half, about 5 minutes.

Combine ricotta, cream and sugar.

Serve warm whole peaches with syrup and ricotta cream.

Tips

• Any remaining syrup can be used to poach more peaches next time.

• For a speedier dessert, halve peaches before poaching and reduce cooking time to 10 minutes.

Prunes and pears cooked in sweetened red wine

Preparation and cooking time: 25 minutes
Serves: 2

1 cup (8 fl oz/250 ml) red wine
1/2 cup (4 oz/125 g) sugar
1/2 cup (4 fl oz/125 ml) water
1 pear, peeled, halved, cored and cut into eights
1 cinnamon stick
2 cardamom pods, crushed
grated zest of 1/2 orange
8 prunes
mascarpone or heavy (double) cream, to serve
wafer cookies, to serve (optional)

Combine wine, sugar and water in saucepan and stir over low heat to dissolve sugar. Bring to a boil and reduce heat to steady simmer.

Add pears, spices and orange zest and simmer for 10 minutes.

Add prunes and cook until prunes are tender and plump, 3 to 4 more minutes. Remove fruit with slotted spoon and bring liquid back to boil. Boil until reduced by half, 3 to 4 minutes.

Pour syrup over pears and prunes. Serve warm with mascarpone and cookies.

Stuffed baked apples

Preparation: 10 minutes
Cooking time: 20 minutes
Serves: 4

4 large cooking apples
1 tablespoon golden raisins (sultanas)
1 tablespoon mixed candied fruit (mixed peel)
2 tablespoons ground almonds
1 tablespoon maple syrup
1 tablespoon orange juice
½ teaspoon ground cloves
1 tablespoon unsalted butter
pinch of nutmeg

Preheat oven to 400°F (200°C/Gas 6). Carefully core apples. Lightly grease baking dish with oil or butter and arrange apples in it.

Combine raisins, candied fruit, almonds, maple syrup, orange juice and cloves in small bowl and mix well. Press mixture into apples; don't worry if filling overflows slightly. Rub butter around tops of apples and sprinkle lightly with nutmeg.

Bake for 20 minutes or until apple skins are shiny and about to burst.

Tips

- This dish is also delicious cold, so make a few extra for the next day and serve with lashings of thick fresh cream.

- When serving hot, let stand for 5 minutes to allow the flavors to infuse.

Summer fruit mélange

Preparation: 15 minutes

Serves: 4

2 grapefruit (pink if in season)

½ cup (4 fl oz/125 ml) apricot nectar

½ teaspoon ground ginger

2 lb (1 kg) piece watermelon

2 large nectarines

10 oz (300 g) apricots

1 basket strawberries (8 oz/250 g)

⅓ cup (3 fl oz/90 ml) heavy (double) cream

2 teaspoons maple syrup

2 teaspoons chopped fresh mint leaves

Cut one grapefruit in half and squeeze out juice. Remove peel and pith from other grapefruit and cut fruit into segments.

Combine juice, nectar and ginger in large bowl and mix well.

Remove rind from watermelon and cut flesh into 1-inch (2.5-cm) pieces. Remove pits (stones) from nectarines and apricots and cut fruit into wedges. Stem and halve strawberries.

Add fruit to juice mixture and toss gently to mix well.

Combine cream and maple syrup in bowl and beat with electric beater until soft peaks form. Stir in mint and chill, if possible.

Top fruit with dollop of minted cream and serve immediately.

Summer fruit sundaes

Preparation: 15 minutes
Serves: 4

2 medium mangoes (1 1/2 lb/625 g)

juice of 1 lime

2 tablespoons superfine (caster) sugar

1 generous cup (9 oz/275 g) curd cheese or small-
   curd cottage cheese

1 1/4 cups (10 fl oz/300 ml) low-fat plain (natural)
   yogurt

1 tablespoon honey

1 teaspoon ground ginger

5 oz (150 g) strawberries, halved

5 oz (150 g) blueberries

Peel mangoes and cut flesh away from pit (stone).
Combine mango, lime juice, sugar and 3/4 of the cheese,
and sugar in blender and puree. Refrigerate.

Combine remaining cheese with 2 tablespoons yogurt to
make thick, creamy mixture; refrigerate. Combine
remaining yogurt with honey and ginger.

Spoon strawberries into four tall sundae or parfait
glasses. Divide 1/2 of the mango mixture among glasses
and top with 1/2 of the sweetened yogurt. Top with
blueberries, then with remaining mango puree and
sweetened yogurt. Spoon dollop of yogurt/cheese
mixture on top.

Tips

• These light desserts are best served really cold, so
  refrigerate for an hour before serving, if time permits.

• This recipe is low in fat, but for a really wicked version,
  use a rich, creamy yogurt, substitute mascarpone for
  curd cheese, and top with grated chocolate.

Glossary

Al dente: an Italian term generally applied to the cooking of pasta. Translated it means "to the tooth", meaning pasta should be firm when bitten, not soft.

Baste: to spoon liquid (usually fat, oil, stock or cooking juices) over food during cooking to prevent drying out, e.g. roast meat and kebabs.

Blanch: commonly used to mean pre-cook or parboil (partially cook) vegetables for a short time so they need little or no further cooking.

Boil: to cook in liquid at boiling point; boiling point of water is 212°F (100°C). The water should be bubbling rapidly, as distinct from simmering (see page 235).

Braise: to cook meat and vegetables by sautéing in fat and then cooking slowly in very little moisture.

Broil (grill): a method of cooking by exposing food to dry heat, either from gas or an electric stove broiler (grill). Is also done using red coals of a barbecue or outdoor fire, or with the surface of a griddle pan heated on a stove or an open fire.

Deep-fry: to cook in a deep, heavy-based pan in sufficient fat or oil to cover food completely. Used for foods requiring a brief time to cook, e.g. fish fillets, French fries and fritters.

Deglaze: to heat liquid (usually stock and/or wine) in a dish or pan, stirring to scrape up sediment that remains after roasting or frying. This forms the base of a sauce.

Degorge: to extract juices from vegetables (e.g. eggplant/aubergine) by salting, then soaking or rinsing, to remove excess moisture or bitter juices. If you prefer not to use salt, soak eggplant (aubergine) for 45 minutes in a large bowl of acidulated water — cold water mixed with the juice of 1 lemon — to achieve similar results. Not all eggplant requires degorging; usually only larger, older specimens.

Dice: to cut meat, cheese or vegetables into small (⅛– ¼ in/ 3–5 mm) or large (1–1⅓ in/2–3 cm) cubes using a sharp knife.

Fold: to combine a light, whisked or creamed mixture with a heavier mixture so that lightness is retained. Use a metal spoon or spatula to cut down through the mixture, across the bottom of the bowl, then up and over, close to the surface — turn the bowl frequently.

Grease (pans, etc.): to use melted butter or oil applied with a brush or buttered paper, or non-stick oil sprays, if preferred, so that what is being cooked does not stick to sides or bottom of pan.

Herbs: to use dried herbs, measure the amount needed onto your hand then crush to release the flavor before adding to a dish. To substitute fresh herbs for dried, double the amount of the fresh.

Julienne: to cut food (e.g. vegetables, citrus rind, ham) into thin matchsticks or very fine shreds.

Marinade: a seasoned mixture (generally of oil and wine) or a sauce with herbs and other flavorings in which meat or fish is left to stand (marinate) for some hours or overnight before cooking. This gives flavor and sometimes tenderizes the food.

Reduce: to boil a mixture, uncovered, until the quantity is reduced and the flavor concentrated.

Refresh: to pass cooked foods, mainly vegetables, quickly under (or immersed in) cold water to stop the cooking process and preserve color.

Sauté: to fry quickly in a shallow pan over high temperature. The food must be completely dry before cooking and cooked in small batches to brown well. A combination of butter and oil is commonly used — butter adds flavor and color and the oil prevents the butter scorching.

Sear: to brown meat quickly on both sides to seal in juices; the heat is usually then lowered for the remaining cooking time.

Seasoned flour: all-purpose (plain) flour to which salt and pepper have been added. Usually used to protect foods from high cooking heats, e.g in frying.

Shallow-fry: to cook in a small quantity of fat or oil in a shallow pan. Used for foods which take a comparatively long time to cook, such as sausages, schnitzels, thick pieces of fish or whole fish.

Simmer: to bring food in liquid to a boil, then to reduce heat and keep the food cooking slowly, just below boiling point, at about 180°F (82°C) so that the liquid bubbles gently. Suitable for casseroles and dishes requiring long, slow cooking.

Skim: to remove scum or fat from the surface of a liquid using a slotted spoon or mesh ladle.

Steam: to cook food in the steam from boiling water, using a perforated utensil, usually made from either bamboo or metal and positioned over the pot or pan of boiling water.

Stir-fry: to cook over high heat, stirring or tossing the food constantly, with a wok spoon (wok chan) in a wok. A large, deep frying pan can also be used.

Sweat: to cook food gently in butter or oil in a tightly covered pan over very low heat. Generally used for vegetables, particularly onions. The slow cooking develops flavor.

Index

Guide to weights & measures

The conversions given in the recipes in this book are approximate. Whichever system you use, remember to follow it consistently, thereby ensuring that the proportions are consistent throughout a recipe.

Weights

Imperial	Metric
1/3 oz	10 g
1/2 oz	15 g
3/4 oz	20 g
1 oz	30 g
2 oz	60 g
3 oz	90 g
4 oz (1/4 lb)	125 g
5 oz (1/3 lb)	150 g
6 oz	180 g
7 oz	220 g
8 oz (1/2 lb)	250 g
9 oz	280 g
10 oz	300 g
11 oz	330 g
12 oz (3/4 lb)	375 g
16 oz (1 lb)	500 g
2 lb	1 kg
3 lb	1.5 kg
4 lb	2 kg

Volume

Imperial	Metric	Cup
1 fl oz	30 ml	
2 fl oz	60 ml	1/4
3 fl oz	90 ml	1/3
4 fl oz	125 ml	1/2
5 fl oz	150 ml	2/3
6 fl oz	180 ml	3/4
8 fl oz	250 ml	1
10 fl oz	300 ml	1 1/4
12 fl oz	375 ml	1 1/2
13 fl oz	400 ml	1 2/3
14 fl oz	440 ml	1 3/4
16 fl oz	500 ml	2
24 fl oz	750 ml	3
32 fl oz	1L	4

Oven temperature guide

The Celsius (°C) and Fahrenheit (°F) temperatures in this chart apply to most electric ovens. Decrease by 25°F or 10°C for a gas oven or refer to the manufacturer's temperature guide. For temperatures below 325°F (160°C), do not decrease the given temperature.

Oven description	°C	°F	Gas Mark
Cool	110	225	1/4
	130	250	1/2
Very slow	140	275	1
	150	300	2
Slow	170	325	3
Moderate	180	350	4
	190	375	5
Moderately Hot	200	400	6
Fairly Hot	220	425	7
Hot	230	450	8
Very Hot	240	475	9
Extremely Hot	250	500	10

Useful conversions

1/4 teaspoon	1.25 ml
1/2 teaspoon	2.5 ml
1 teaspoon	5 ml
1 Australian tablespoon	20 ml (4 teaspoons)
1 UK/US tablespoon	15 ml (3 teaspoons)

Butter/Shortening

1 tablespoon	1/2 oz	15 g
1 1/2 tablespoons	3/4 oz	20 g
2 tablespoons	1 oz	30 g
3 tablespoons	1 1/2 oz	45 g

A LANSDOWNE BOOK

First published by Apple Press in the UK in 2006
Sheridan House
4th Floor
114 Western Road
Hove
East Sussex BN3 1DD
United Kingdom

www.apple-press.com

Copyright © 2004 text, photographs and design: Lansdowne Publishing Pty Ltd 2004

Created and produced by Lansdowne Publishing Pty Ltd
Level 1, 18 Argyle St, Sydney NSW 2000, Australia
www.lansdownepublishing.com.au

Text: Myles Beaufort, Nicole Gaunt, Suzie Smith, Kirsten Tilgals, Linda Venturoni-Wilson
Photography: John Hollingshead, Rowan Fotheringham
Designer: Grant Slaney, The Modern Art Production Group
Production Manager: Sally Stokes
Editor: Joanne Holliman
Project Co-ordinator: Kate Merrifield

ISBN-10: 1 84543 125 1
ISBN-13: 978 1 84543 125 9

All rights reserved. No part of this publication may be reproduced,
stored in a retrieval system, or transmitted in any form, or by any means,
electronic, mechanical, photocopying, recording, or otherwise, without
the prior written permission of the publisher.

Set in Helvetica on QuarkXPress
Printed in Singapore by Tien Wah Press (Pte) Ltd.